Being a
Progressive
Christian
(is ˄ not) *for*
Dummies
(nor for kn˄ow-it-alls)

AN EVOLUTION OF FAITH

Chuck Queen

© 2013

Published in the United States by Nurturing Faith Inc., Macon GA,
www.nurturingfaith.net.

Library of Congress Cataloging-in-Publication Data is available.

978-1-938514-38-8

Contents

Introduction...v

Chapter 1: But the Bible Says . . . (Scripture)

What the Bible Says Is Not Necessarily What God Says 3
The Bible Is Not an Answer Book 5
Reading Scripture Transformatively...7
Hearing the Divine Voice 9
How Jesus Read His Bible 11
Experience Generally Trumps Tradition...13
Honoring Sacred Texts 15

Chapter 2: "Hey, I'm a Believer Now" (Faith)

Who Are You: Saint or Sinner? 19
When the Old-Time Religion No Longer Works..............................20
The Essence of an Inclusive Faith 22
Faithfulness Is More Important Than Veneration 24
Openness to a Larger Vision...26
Discovering a Living Faith..28
Taste and See That God is Good 30

Chapter 3: A New Way for a New Day (Christianity)

Christianity Is a Way of Life...35
Toxic Christianity..36
Let the Church Be the Church 38
Christianity Must Lose Its Dualism 40
Hope for the Evangelical Church 42
The Myth of Redemptive Violence...44
Three Keys to Transformative Christianity 47

Chapter 4: "Redeemed, How I Love to Proclaim It" (Salvation)

Salvation Is Now 53
The Cure for Possession 55
Salvation Is about Life Change 57
Conversion Is Possible 59
Is God's Kingdom a Real Possibility? 61
God's Loving Judgment 63
Wendell Berry and the Afterlife 66

Chapter 5: Walking the Talk (Discipleship)

Followers of the Way 71
Joel Osteen and the Scandalous Gospel of Jesus 73
God May Make Christians of Us Yet 76
God Suffers with Our Suffering World 78
Discovering Our True Vocation 80
Finding Our Rhythm 82
Stages of Spiritual Struggle 84

Chapter 6: The Upside-Down Kingdom (Beatitudes)

What Possesses Us? 89
Living with Grief and Joy 90
Meekness Is Not Weakness 92
Hungering for Justice 94
Swimming in God's Mercy 97
Pursuing God's New World 99
Called To Be Peacemakers 102

Recommended Reading..105

Introduction

The progressive Christian movement occurring within Western Christianity has invaded both conservative and liberal ranks. As we evolve in spiritual consciousness as a species, we must continually critique, revise, and reformulate our belief systems. The following reflections challenge a number of traditional Christian teachings and images, while developing some fresh, progressive perspectives. All reconstruction requires some deconstruction, and while I engage in both, the reflections in this book have an overall positive tone that nurtures a vision of Christian faith that, I hope, the reader will find attractive and compelling.

I trust that the criticisms I articulate do not reflect in any way a stance of spiritual elitism or superiority, for such attitudes have no place in the kind of Christianity I am advocating. In theological and biblical discussions and debates it is my practice to say: This is my current perspective—where I am now on my faith journey. That will, no doubt, change. I could be wrong. I am sure I am wrong about a good number of things.

I do not claim any special access to or possession of the truth. But I know that any positive way forward requires two things: a rigorous critique of one's past and current faith heritage and tradition, and a thoughtful formulation of a positive vision for renewal and change. I have tried to maintain a balance between tearing down and building up. Whether or not I have achieved this balance, the reader will have to decide.

My critique focuses on some of the fundamental positions of conservative, evangelical Christianity because that is my heritage and where my journey began. I'm sure progressive Christians who were schooled in the old, classical liberalism could bring just as rigorous a critique to that tradition. My first two academic degrees were from staunchly conservative Christian schools where faculty members were required to teach within narrowly defined parameters that espoused such doctrines as biblical inerrancy and substitutionary atonement. I do not, however, disparage my conservative Christian training. It gave me the strong foundation I needed for that stage in my life, and I am certain I would not be where I am today without those structures and boundaries.

My Bible college training taught me the Scriptures. As part of the curriculum, we worked our way through the entire Bible. Obviously, we brought our traditional biases and presuppositions into this process, but I was required to spend a lot of time in the biblical text itself and thus learned the basic content of the Bible.

Ironically, my studies in a conservative seminary gave me the tools to self-critique conservative doctrines and beliefs. In particular, a class on New Testament textual criticism crystallized a shift in my thinking that began to emerge from my elective courses in New Testament Greek exegesis. I was surprised to learn about the different character of the New Testament manuscripts, the sheer number of variants in those manuscripts, and the subjective process involved in evaluating the external and internal evidence of each variant in order to make a reasonable guess about the original wording. I was also surprised to learn how many variants were intentional—the result of scribal deletions, additions, and alterations to the text in order to support a particular view or interpretation.

Textual critical study was emphasized because of the importance the seminary leadership placed on determining the text of the original autographs, which in their view was inerrant. I reasoned: If it is virtually impossible to determine with any certitude the original reading in a vast number of cases, then why did God not guide the text transmission process to make clear the original reading? Why did God not guarantee the preservation of the inerrant reading, if God went to all the trouble to inspire the original text in the first place? Thus began my questioning of the traditional Christian paradigm.

By the time I enrolled in the Doctor of Ministry program at Southern Baptist Theological Seminary in Louisville, Kentucky, I had abandoned belief in the inerrancy of the original autographs. At the time, Southern Seminary was still a highly respected theological school, blending both conservative and progressive elements. That would soon change with the fundamentalist takeover of the Southern Baptist Convention. After I received my degree in 1993 and a new president was appointed, there was a mass exodus of moderate and progressive professors. The once highly acclaimed and applauded moderate school, known for its unique capacity to hold conservative and liberal perspectives in tension, devolved into a kind of glorified Bible institute. Many former students and professors are still grieving the loss two decades later.

One of the reasons there was such a fertile field within Southern Baptist churches for conservatives to plant and harvest their political and theological agendas was because of the failure of pastors trained in progressive Christian hermeneutics, theology, and spirituality to inform and teach their congregations what they had learned in seminary. Most churches, before the takeover, had both conservative and moderate members, but even in congregations where moderates outnumbered conservatives there was still a strong reluctance from pastors to teach what they knew about the nature of

Scripture, the process of theological reflection, and historical-critical methods of interpretation. Many pastors feared the wrath of their conservative members who tended to be more dogmatic and outspoken than moderates. It was not vocationally safe to stir up the waters with the truth, and the truth suffered.

In my reflection, "Hope for the Evangelical Church," I call attention to the way Rob Bell, a former mega-church pastor and the author of *Love Wins*, has revolted against this trend. While he still refuses to be identified as a progressive, rejecting and despising all labels, he has certainly embraced many of the core convictions of progressive Christianity. James K. Wellman Jr. has written a fascinating account of Bell's journey. He quotes emergent church leader Tony Jones, who in early 2011 predicted what would happen with Bell as a result of his release of *Love Wins*:

> The Calvinistas will attack Rob as a universalist. Rob won't care. *Christianity Today* will write a review that expresses some serious doubt and hesitation about Rob's new book, but they won't entirely throw him under the bus (yet). Rob won't care. Lots of people, like me, will blog about this. Rob won't care. Some people will even leave Mars Hill Church because they don't like what's in the book. Rob won't care.[1]

If the progressive Christian movement is to have a measurable impact upon American Christianity, it will take more pastors like Rob Bell who are willing to teach their congregations that healthy, transformative Christianity is a journey that leads to new places and fuels ever new and evolving questions in pursuit of truth. It most certainly will involve more small-town pastors, like myself, who will dare to elevate the pursuit and proclamation of truth above their professional careers.

This work consists of six chapters that explore the following themes from a progressive Christian viewpoint: Scripture, faith, Christianity, salvation, discipleship, and the Beatitudes. Each reflection is followed by a section titled "Going Deeper" that includes questions for personal reflection and group discussion. Though each reflection is complete in itself, the reflections are arranged in each chapter so that they build on each other, adding to the development of the theme. They weave together personal experiences and vignettes from literature and film, with creative biblical interpretation and theological exposition.

There are several ways to benefit from reading this book. Because each reflection stands on its own, one could use this as a devotional book, reading one reflection each day or however one chooses. The questions in the "Going Deeper" section can be used to provoke thoughtful reflection on the topic or perspective presented. These questions provide an excellent resource for church discipleship and study groups, or any reading group interested in exploring progressive Christian themes. Study group leaders can decide what questions to utilize. The format allows great flexibility for personal reading and reflection, as well as for study and discipleship groups.

These reflections are written with the intent of being intellectually stimulating, emotionally evoking, theologically substantive, and practically helpful. They are designed to stir the imagination, spark critical thinking, and nurture Christian faith and spirituality. Most of all, they are intended to ignite new questions that will inspire the reader to explore, think, and embrace the mystery and wonder of the Christian spiritual path. Thomas Merton said, "In the progress toward religious understanding, one does not go from answer to answer but from question to question. One's questions are answered, not by clear, definitive answers, but by more pertinent and more crucial questions."[2] It is my hope that this book will lead the reader to ask "more pertinent and more crucial questions."

Notes

[1]Tony Jones, "What's Up with Rob Bell?" http://www.patheos.com/blogs/tony-jones/2011/02/28/whats-up-with-rob-bell/ (February 28, 2011). Referenced by James K. Wellman, Jr., *Rob Bell and a New American Christianity* (Nashville: Abingdon Press, 2012), 22.

[2]Thomas Merton, *Opening the Bible* (Collegeville, MN: The Liturgical Press, 1970), 29-30.

CHAPTER 1

But the Bible Says ...

(Scripture)

What the Bible Says Is Not Necessarily What God Says

It takes spiritual eyes to read the Bible in a healthy, transformative way. The Bible can be (and has been) employed as an instrument of oppression and evil, as well as an instrument of change and transformation. Almost all Christians who struggle with issues of faith and spirituality individually, in the Christian community or in a public forum, rely upon their understanding and interpretation of Scripture as a major component in arriving at their conclusions. Whether the issue is related to sexual orientation, women pastors or deacons, the role of government, the right to wage war, the role of the military, divorce, the nature of Jesus, or the nature of judgment and salvation, Scripture is generally quoted and referenced by all Christians engaged in discussion and debate. The critical questions involve how we use and interpret Scripture, what framework and guiding principles we employ to make sense of Scripture, and how we apply it to our lives and communities.

Some years ago I, along with three other pastors, tried to change the policy regarding women's participation in an Eastern Kentucky Baptist Association of the Southern Baptist Convention. As the policy stood, women could not speak publicly to any issue up for a vote at the annual meeting. It's hard to believe such policies are still in place, but as far as I know, such is still the policy in that Baptist association. An amendment was presented, and I spoke on its behalf. I appealed to passages in the Gospels showing how Jesus was egalitarian and inclusive in his ministry and mission, calling women disciples (Luke 8:1-3). I talked about the social vision of God's new creation expounded by Paul in Galatians—how that "in Christ" all social, sexual, and racial barriers are abolished (3:27-28). I pointed to Scriptures demonstrating that women served as coworkers and partners with Paul in preaching and teaching the gospel (Rom. 16:1-2, 7; Phil. 4:2-3).

Do you know what happened? Those who opposed the change also quoted Scripture. They quoted 1 Corinthians 14:34 that says women should be silent and subordinate in the church, and if they have anything to say they should ask their husbands at home. Someone asked, "What if they don't have husbands?" Their response was, "They need to get husbands." This led to the oppressive text in 1 Timothy 2:11-14 that says women should "learn in silence with full submission" and must not be permitted "to teach or to have authority over a man." The theological rationale given by the writer plays on the supposed order of creation and the moral inferiority of the woman: "For Adam was formed first, then Eve; and Adam was not deceived, but the woman was deceived and became a transgressor." It's in the Bible, they said. And they were right, of course; it is in the Bible.

And what the Bible says, God says, right? I don't know of anything that has done more harm in and to the church than this simple equation: What the Bible says is equal to what God says. The direct identification of God's voice with what the Bible says has been used to justify all sorts of destructive biases and oppressive practices. Think of all the preachers who raise their voices declaring, "The Bible says . . ." assuming this is what God says. This practice has done immense damage.

In the story of Jesus' transfiguration in the Synoptic Gospels, Moses and Elijah (representatives of the Law and the Prophets) appear with Jesus (see Luke 9:28-36). But it is Jesus alone who is affirmed by the divine voice: "This is my Son, my Chosen; listen to him." The point made is that the Law and the Prophets find fulfillment in Jesus. Listen to Jesus, the voice declares.

Here is the key to a holistic, healthy, and transformative Christian reading of the Bible: Jesus is the lens through which Christians see. A truly constructive, redemptive, and transformative Christian reading of Scripture filters our understanding of the biblical stories and writings through the ultimate story, the story of Jesus. This means that an authentic Christian reading will always be tilted and biased toward the things Jesus embodied, taught, and died for, such as reconciling peace, restorative justice, inclusive forgiveness, purity of heart, and love of enemy—to name the more essential things.

Going Deeper

1. Have you ever found yourself embarrassed by how some Christians use the Bible in oppressive ways? In your estimation, what are some destructive uses of the Bible?

2. What's the difference between saying "the Bible is the Word of God" and "the Bible can become the Word of God" and "the Bible is a witness to the Word of God"? Why does it matter?

3. There is some circular reasoning involved in arguing that Jesus is the lens through which we should read the Bible. Obviously, we are dependent upon the Gospels for a reliable portrait of Jesus. Given the nature of the Gospels as documents combining memory with creative theological proclamation and interpretation, do you think they can be trusted for painting a reliable picture of Jesus of Nazareth? Why or why not?

The Bible Is Not an Answer Book

One day I received an e-mail from a representative of SONday Distributors. The company had a special deal "for churches only" on "a great Bible." For just ten dollars each (regular forty-dollar value) we could get a shipment of ANSWER Bibles. That's right—the ANSWER Bible. Their goal, she wrote, was "to plant a Bible (I presume she meant an ANSWER Bible) in 10,000 homes, organizations, and establishments in communities across America." She wanted churches to make a commitment to give them away to "lost" people.

This approach is typical of dualistic versions of Christianity. It's always "the other" who is "lost" and needs what I have. I'm the answer man or woman. I've got the truth, brother. We have the answers, sister. Find it here! Amen!

Normally I click "delete," not giving this sort of thing a second glance, but for some reason I couldn't resist the temptation to be a bit sarcastic. (This was not one of my best days.) So I shot back an e-mail to the sales representative: "No thanks, Paula (not her real name; I'm protecting the guilty). I've heard enough ANSWERS in my day, but if you ever get a Bible that invites people to ask the hard QUESTIONS let me know." She responded with a stinging reprimand, ending the e-mail with: "I say this with the love of Jesus in me." I couldn't not respond (with the love of Jesus in me, of course).

Personally, I think if we are going to just pass out Bibles randomly, we should at least attach a warning label: "This could be hazardous to your health." What I have discovered is that people looking for answers in the Bible tend to find the answers they are looking for. We all have a tendency to project the answers we want to find into the biblical text.

When we approach a biblical text, we bring our biases with us. It's unavoidable. The biblical authors and communities were no different than us; they, too, were children of their culture. Their faith encounters with the divine were interpreted within the framework of their presuppositions, beliefs, and worldview. Sometimes their experience reshaped their beliefs and worldview, but there can be no denial of the powerful influence of tradition and culture through which all of us filter our experience.

There are many transformative texts in the sacred Scriptures, but there are also a few oppressive texts, and often these can be found in the same biblical book (compare 1 Corinthians 13 with 1 Cor. 14:34-35).

The key question that I believe every disciple of Jesus must bring to the Bible is this: Does the text bear witness to the gospel? Does the Scripture bear witness to the unconditional love of God and the universal call to restorative justice embodied in the life, teachings, death, and resurrection of Christ?

Much of the time our sacred Scriptures do indeed bear witness to the gospel in varying degrees, but other times the meaning of the gospel is distorted. Sometimes, disciples of Jesus who seek to live the gospel of Christ must stand in opposition to the biblical text.

The Bible is not an answer book, but it can prompt us to ask the right questions if we approach it honestly, openly, and truthfully, grounded in the inclusive love and restorative justice of Christ.

We all bring our presuppositions and assumptions with us into the interpretative process. This was just as true for the biblical authors and communities as it is for us; it's part of the human condition. We cannot eliminate our biases, but if we are honest enough to acknowledge that we have them, our study of the Bible is then more likely to prompt us to ask the right questions instead of offering us shallow answers. With a more humble approach to the Bible, it can be employed as a tool for transformation rather than as an instrument of oppression.

Going Deeper

1. Why is it that "people looking for answers in the Bible tend to find the answers they are looking for"? Franciscan priest and author Richard Rohr likes to say: "Most people see things as *they* are, rather than as they *are*." How much impact does one's place in history, family of origin, faith tradition, genetics, cultural influence, etc. have on the way that person reads and interprets the Bible?

2. We all read and interpret the Scriptures with some degree of bias. Our understanding is influenced by the presuppositions and prejudices we bring with us to the interpretative process. Can you name some of yours?

3. Why are there oppressive texts in the Bible that seem to stand in opposition to the gospel of Jesus? What does that say about the biblical authors, editors, and communities responsible for these texts? How might this affect one's understanding of biblical inspiration and authority? Do you think there are levels or degrees of inspiration?

Reading Scripture Transformatively

New Testament scholar Marcus Borg shared a wonderful story illustrating two different ways to approach Scripture. For many years Borg taught an introductory-level Bible course at Oregon State University. At the beginning of the class he always informed the students that the course would be taught from the perspective of the academic discipline of biblical scholarship. Borg would tell them they didn't have to change their beliefs, but to do well in the class they would have to be willing to look at the Bible from that viewpoint.

He explained that the Bible is the product of two ancient communities: the Hebrew Bible of ancient Israel, and the Christian Testament of the early Christian movement. As such, the Bible tells us not how God sees things, but how those two ancient communities saw their relationship with God.

Roughly twenty percent of the students who took the course believed that the Bible was inerrant (literally the Word of God). Borg would, inevitably, spend the first two weeks in lively discussion with the more articulate and courageous of those students.

One semester, a very bright Muslim engineering student took the course. A senior, he did so because he needed another humanities course for graduation and the class fit his schedule. One day, after witnessing Borg's interaction with the more conservative students, the young Muslim said to Borg, "I think I understand what's going on. You're saying the Bible is like a lens through which we see God, and they're saying that it's important to believe in the lens."[1]

That is a good analogy. When I am asked if I believe the Bible, my response is: As a Christian, I trust in the living Christ and follow the way of Jesus of Nazareth. I read and interpret the Bible as a means of nurturing a transformative relationship with God, whom I know through Jesus. The Bible is a lens through which I see God and Jesus.

I try to be open to both the diversity and the unity of faith the various authors and faith communities express. I try to be receptive to both the contradictions and the coherences, the discontinuity and continuity found in the many different kinds of sacred literature in the Bible.

When the Bible becomes the object of faith (bibliolatry?), the Bible can easily become an instrument of oppression and death. In a general sense, the Bible gives us a description of the faith of the writers and communities expressed through diverse genres as they struggled with what is real and unreal, not a set of infallible prescriptions or propositions.

Every reading of the Bible is an interpretation of the Bible. The reader inevitably brings his or her temperament, personality, spirituality, culture, biases, and education into the process of understanding the text and discerning its meaning for today. It's good to remember the old adage: Every viewpoint is a view from a point.

The Bible is not just about God but about how people of faith have perceived and related to God. While it is not literally the Word of God, it can become the Word of God (the divine voice speaks through it) to those who read it critically, spiritually, and discerningly. We should employ the best methods at our disposal to make sense of it. This should include a balance between the best resources of historical-critical scholarship and other methods more spiritually oriented toward nurturing Christian disciples, such as *Lectio divina* (an ancient contemplative practice involving the repetitive reading of the Bible interspersed with periods of silence).

The Bible contains a plurality of voices; sometimes these voices conflict with one another, sometimes they speak as one, using different language and words. The Bible includes voices of oppression (claiming to speak for God) and voices of protest against oppression (also claiming to speak for God). There are voices that endorse conventional wisdom and voices that speak a subversive, alternative wisdom. But in, with, around, under, and over these voices is the divine voice, seeking to lead us into a transformative relationship with our creator and redeemer.

Going Deeper

1. I said in a previous reflection that Jesus is the lens through which Christians should read the Bible. Now I am saying that the Bible is the lens through which we see God and Jesus. How are these two statements similar, and how are they different? In what ways are they helpful, and in what ways are they inadequate?

2. What are the dangers of bibliolatry, or making the Bible the object of faith?

3. How do you know when the Bible becomes the Word of God to you personally and communally (within the church, the faith community)?

4. Do you think the distinction made between the Bible and "the divine voice" is helpful or confusing? Are there ways and means through which the divine voice speaks to receptive minds and hearts other than through the Bible? Can you share a personal experience when you felt you heard the divine voice? How did it impact you?

Hearing the Divine Voice

In my final year of seminary I was pastor of a small rural church in a little Indiana farm community. This was a seminary pastorate; the church didn't expect me to stay after graduation, and I didn't expect to stay. As graduation drew close, I was ready to go on to bigger and better things. The problem was that no one else seemed ready for me to go on to bigger and better things. I had sent out résumés—no response, not even a nibble. Churches were not exactly knocking on my door wanting me to come. In fact, they were not even sending me any rejection letters. This process went on for several months. I began to question my calling. At one point I was so filled with anxiety that I found it difficult to sit in class. I felt miserable and felt guilty for feeling so miserable. And the feelings of guilt for doubting my calling and questioning my faith compounded my anxiety.

I happened to be taking a pastoral counseling class at the time, and the professor said something very simple that struck me as quite profound. It came to me as a word from God. He said, "It's okay to feel bad." Pretty simple isn't it? But that is what I needed to hear. An immense weight lifted when I appropriated that word.

Some of the anxiety I was experiencing came from the sense that my stay in Hoover, Indiana, could be for a longer time than I had wanted or antici-pated. But the debilitating, oppressive anxiety I felt crushing me sprang from the guilt over feeling bad and from questioning my calling. When I realized it was okay to feel bad, to question and to experience some anxiety, then the deep dread, guilt, and worry that hovered over me started to dissipate.

I share this story as an illustration of how the divine voice can speak to us. It often speaks through human words, images, ideas, and feelings. This communication frequently occurs in communal contexts. In our privatized, individualized culture we need to be reminded that the sacred documents of the Bible emerged out of faith communities and were written to faith communities. So as the community gathers for worship, prayer, fellowship, study, and service, the community can expect to hear God speak.

Paul tells the church in Corinth to "weigh carefully" what the Christian prophets proclaim in their worship gatherings (1 Cor. 14:29). He tells the church at Thessalonica to "test everything" proclaimed by the prophets and teachers in their community, holding on to what is good and avoiding all that is evil (1 Thess. 5:19-22).

The divine voice often speaks healing and transforming words as Scripture is read, interpreted, discussed, taught, and proclaimed in Christian communities. But biblical words read and interpreted must be "weighed carefully." The Bible can just as easily be used to justify our sexism, racism, classism, nationalism, and egotism as it can be used for redemption and transformation. There is no infallible word. Here are some questions I ask:

- Do the words reflect the compassion, love, forgiveness, and prophetic challenge of Christ?
- Do the words inspire hearers to be more caring, empathetic, gracious, hospitable, and inclusive?
- Do the words challenge the status quo, confront conventional wisdom, and envisage an alternative world that calls forth risky compassion?
- Do the words bring out the best of the human spirit?
- Do the words inspire us to pursue peace, reconciliation, and justice for all people, especially the disadvantaged and marginalized?
- Do the words bring healing in a holistic sense, calling forth humility, generosity, gratitude, and grace?

Paul writes to the church in Rome that "the Spirit bears witness with our spirit that we are the children of God" (Rom. 8:16). When our lives are immersed and filled with the Spirit of Christ, it is not that difficult to discern the divine voice bearing witness to our human spirit. When our lives are not filled with the Spirit of Christ, we will often mishear the voice, as I can testify through my own experience. Some Christians who mishear that voice seek to justify their prejudices and sin by appealing to an infallible Bible.

Every voice in the Bible or in the church should be filtered through and weighed against the divine voice that has become incarnate in Jesus of Nazareth, the Word made flesh, full of grace and truth (John 1:1-18).

Going Deeper

1. In the above piece I shared a personal story of how I encountered the divine voice through the words of a seminary professor. What sort of impact should one look for and expect in discerning the voice of God?

2. Read 1 Corinthians 14:1-33. In this passage Paul argues that the exercise of the gift of prophecy is more valuable to the Corinthian community than the practice of the gift of tongues. Without becoming too distracted by the details of this passage (which can be difficult to understand), what is the gist of Paul's emphasis on the benefit and value of prophecy for the Corinthian church? Could the same or similar criteria be applied in contemporary church settings to discern the voice of God?

3. Why do you think so many Christians long for and grasp after an infallible word? How might a Christian community go about "carefully weighing" that which claims or sounds like a word from God?

4. What might be the theological significance and the spiritual implications of identifying Jesus with the "Word" in the prologue of John's Gospel (1:1-18)?

How Jesus Read His Bible

When teaching his disciples to love their enemies, Jesus grounds his instruction in the nature of God: "If you love those who love you, what credit is that to you? . . . But love your enemies, do good, and lend, expecting nothing in return. Your reward will be great, and you will be children of the Most High; for he is kind to the ungrateful and the wicked. Be merciful, just as your Father is merciful" (Luke 6:32-36). Disciples of Jesus must love their enemies because God loves God's enemies.

Where did Jesus get this? He seems to be building on the teaching of the Torah: "Love your neighbor as yourself." But what compels him to make this leap to include the enemy as one's neighbor?

Jesus doesn't arrive at this conclusion from simply reading his Bible. Certainly there is no shortage of stories and teachings in the Hebrew Bible that speak of God's longsuffering and steadfast love, particularly in connection with God's covenant people. From time to time in the Hebrew Bible a more universal perspective breaks through. The book of Jonah poignantly reflects God's love for the enemy. But then, there is also much biblical material that contradicts Jesus' admonition to love one's enemies.

Jesus' ethical teaching appears to be primarily based on his own personal experience of God, whom he calls *Abba* (Father, Mother, Caring One). Jesus' radical teaching to love one's enemies emerges from his own personal experience of divine compassion.

So while Jesus is well-versed in Scripture and has a great respect for the Bible and the traditions of his religious heritage, he is not bound by his faith tradition. This is why in the Gospels we see Jesus constantly challenging some rather popular and widespread Jewish beliefs and practices, rejecting some and in other cases offering new, fresh interpretations and perspectives. For example, in Matthew's version of "love your enemies," Jesus introduces the instruction by setting it against common, conventional biblical teaching: "You have heard it said, 'Love your neighbor and hate your enemy.' But I tell you . . ." (see Matt. 6:43-48).

Jesus reads his Bible and interprets his tradition through the filter of his own radical experience of divine love. The intimate relationship Jesus sustains with his *Abba* (which is poetically expounded so beautifully in the Gospel of John) provides a grid for reading, interpreting, and applying his traditions.

God is a mystery, and while the mystery has been made known to us in Jesus of Nazareth (as well as in other ways) God is not a subject we can study with scientific accuracy. Yet, many Christians treat the Bible like a microscope through which they look to label, name, and define God.

Why do we do this? Most would not admit it, but I think it arises out of a subconscious need to make God manageable. Our reading and inter-pretation of the Bible, if we are not careful, can simply be a way to use God for our benefit. Think of how many Christians have attempted to use God (based on their narrow reading of the Bible) to give them victory over their enemies (in direct contradiction to the life and teaching of Jesus), whether the enemy be a nation, terrorist group, political party or candidate, religious group, or sports team.

Many of us Christians have used the Bible to domesticate Jesus and make him fit neatly into our belief system in order that we might feel safe and secure. It's much easier to retreat within a fortress of "us" versus "them" religion, promising "us" heaven and "the others" hell, than to bother with this messy business of forgiveness and loving our enemies, which is extremely hard work.

Many of us are living with deeply entrenched illusions. But the good news is that the living, cosmic Christ, who defies confinement and explodes categories, who is present in every person, every community, and all creation, is in the business of shattering our illusions.

Going Deeper

1. I suggest that Jesus read his Bible (the Hebrew Scriptures) through the filter of his personal experience of God as *Abba* (Loving Parent). Do you think this is a legitimate way for us to read our Bibles? Do you think this is a reliable guide in determining which Scriptures have authority for the life of Christian discipleship?

2. Because Jesus trusted his experience of God to inform his reading of Scripture and his appropriation of his Jewish tradition, he found himself both in continuity/agreement and in discontinuity/disagreement with his tradition. Have you ever questioned your religious heritage (beliefs and

practices) because of your experience of God? If so, in what ways? If not, can you imagine how an encounter with the divine might cause you to question some of your ideas, beliefs, and interpretations of Scripture?

3. Do you agree with the suggestion that some of our interpretations of Scripture reflect our desire to manage God? Can you name some ways you have attempted to manage God?

4. What do you think about the statement that "the living, cosmic Christ . . . is present in every person, every community, and all creation"? How might Christ be present in an "evil doer"?

Experience Generally Trumps Tradition

Three times in the book of Acts, Paul's experience of his encounter with the living Christ is told. In Acts 9, Luke, as the narrator, tells the story. In Acts 22, Luke has Paul recount his experience to an unruly temple crowd. And in Acts 26, Luke has Paul retell his experience to Festus and King Agrippa. Paul's own brief account of his encounter with Christ is found in Galatians 1:13-17. Paul explains this experience as a revelation— "God was pleased . . . to reveal his Son to me"—and as a calling through grace "to proclaim Christ among the Gentiles."

Paul says that after this encounter he did not "confer with any human being," nor did he go up to Jerusalem to get the endorsement of the Twelve ("those who were already apostles before me"). Instead, he goes to Arabia, and then afterward to Damascus where he begins proclaiming that Jesus is the Messiah. We don't know how long he is in Arabia.

As a result of this experience, Paul undergoes a change from being a Pharisee, who persecutes Jewish followers of Jesus, to a self-pronounced apostle of Jesus, whom he now proclaims to be the Messiah. Paul's hatred for Jesus' disciples is converted through his experience of Jesus to a love for all humanity.

Scholars of Paul, while noting he was a very complex person, marked by both glaring contradictions and shades of brilliance, are, for the most part, in agreement that he was forever changed by his dramatic experience of the living Christ.

Paul bases his authority as an apostle on that experience. His experience of the living Christ takes preeminence over every external authority, including the Hebrew Scriptures. In fact, Paul reinterprets the Scriptures in light of his mystical experience of Christ.

Paul, however, still values his religious tradition. He always considers himself to be a Jewish follower of the Messiah. He never claims to be a Christian in the way the word is used today by most Christians.

We know that Paul values the traditions of Jesus that were passed down orally, because he tells the Corinthians that he passed on to them the gospel tradition of Jesus' death and resurrection he "had received" (see 1 Cor. 15:3-11).

Yet, in this passage, he grounds his own apostleship, not on the tradition he had received, but on his personal experience of the living Christ, who appeared to him as "last of all [the apostles], as to one untimely born" (1 Cor. 15:8).

The lesson we can learn is this: Paul's experience of the living Christ always takes priority and precedence over his tradition and every external authority, even the Bible itself.

Healthy and transformative spirituality will generally always value the divine-human experience over tradition, even the tradition passed on through our sacred texts. The tradition and the sacred texts are important, but one's actual experience of the divine love and goodness that Christians see incarnated in Jesus of Nazareth is more important.

It takes an encounter with divine love to transform our prejudices, jealousies, resentments, and hate into forgiveness and redemption. Such encounters are always more important than what the preachers and dogmatists tell us the Bible says.

Going Deeper

1. In many of the formulations proposed for rightly interpreting Scripture and discerning God's will, four components are often included: reason, tradition, experience, and common sense. I have elevated experience as the most important component. Do you agree or disagree? Why? What do you value most?

2. In 1 Corinthians 15:1-11, to what does Paul attribute his conversion/call? Did he come by this through the Christian tradition or through experience? For most of us it is a combination of tradition and experience. What was the process through which you came to faith?

3. How might we test our spiritual experience to know whether it is truly of God? Is it possible to be certain? What does authentic God experience look like? What sort of thoughts, emotions, feelings, responses, and actions are produced by genuine God experience?

4. In Galatians 3:8-9, 16 how does Paul reinterpret the Hebrew Scripture in light of his experience and understanding of the Christ event? Should our present experience of Christ lead us to reinterpret New Testament texts?

Honoring Sacred Texts

On September 11, 2010, at Highland Baptist Church in Louisville, Kentucky, I attended a service called "Honoring Sacred Texts." The service included representatives from the Christian, Jewish, Muslim, Hindu, Buddhist, Sikh, and Baha'i communities, each reading a selection from their sacred texts. According to Joe Phelps, senior pastor of Highland, it was intended "to be a word of witness against . . . divisive hate-filled ideology, found in every nation and religion, by reading what we believe is fundamental and common from our various sacred texts: love, humility, peace, reverence before the Creator."

Phelps and the good folks at Highland Baptist Church took plenty of heat for this courageous action. Rev. Phelps wrote on his blog that their intent was not in any way "to deny or dilute the role of Jesus, who is central to the message and mission of Highland." He then observed that the way of Jesus was "one of reconciling love rather than polarizing division," and that the only ones Jesus excluded were "driven by a spirit of division."

Phelps noted that "while there are passages that say he [Jesus] is the only way to God . . . other Bible passages are clear that God's bigness and love extend to all the earth, to all peoples, to all nations who come in reverence before God." See, for example, passages such as Acts 10:34-35, Eph. 1:9-10, Col. 1:19-20, and 1 Cor. 15:22. Phelps wrote, "Every sacred text—including the Bible—has passages that extol violence, which can be misunderstood and misapplied by outsiders (and by insiders)."

Our sacred text, the Bible, argues with itself in numerous places. In an internet conversation with a Christian who refused to identify himself, I pointed out several passages of Scripture where there are clear contradictions and asked him to explain or defend his inerrant position on the Bible in light of these discrepancies. That ended the conversation. He apparently didn't want to tackle the impossible.

It seems to me that the Christians who are most in "denial" of the faith are those who, like my internet friend, are actually incapable of offering a legitimate, credible defense of the inconsistencies and contradictions in our sacred text. Claiming the Bible's infallibility possibly turns more thinking young people away from Christianity than any other doctrine of conservative Christianity.

I love our sacred text, but I do not worship it. I probably spend more time and effort studying it and teaching it than most do who claim that it is the literal word of God. While I regard it as divinely inspired, it is clear to me that it is not without human flaws and errors. Rev. Phelps observed that the Christian's sacred text is a diverse "collection of inspirations and understandings which must be allowed to interact and inform each other."

I am convinced that a healthy, transformative, compassion-filled Christianity is directly connected to an interpretation of Scripture that is rooted and grounded in the inclusive gospel of Jesus Christ.[2] Thank goodness I am not alone. There are a number of other Christian leaders and churches like Rev. Phelps and Highland Baptist Church (and more are emerging) who are committed to preaching, teaching, and sharing God's unconditional love as expressed in the inclusive gospel of Jesus of Nazareth.

Going Deeper

1. Do you believe that God speaks through the sacred texts of other religious faiths? Why or why not?

2. John 14:6 and Acts 4:12 suggest that Jesus is the only way to God. Could these texts be interpreted and understood in a different way? Compare Acts 4:12 with Acts 10:34-35. Is this a place where the Bible "argues with itself"?

3. Do you think there is an essential core to the gospel of Jesus that should guide, inform, and correct our reading and interpretation of Scripture? In your view what constitutes that "essential core"?

Notes

[1]Marcus Borg and N. T. Wright, *The Meaning of Jesus: Two Visions* (New York: HarperCollins, 1999), 238-39.

[2]For those interested in further elaboration of my understanding of what constitutes the inclusive gospel of Christ, see my book, *A Faith Worth Living: The Dynamics of an Inclusive Gospel* (Eugene, OR: Resource Publications, 2011).

CHAPTER 2

"Hey, I'm a Believer Now"

(Faith)

Who Are You: Saint or Sinner?

William Sloane Coffin, a few years before his death, wrote a wonderful book titled, *Letters to a Young Doubter*. At the beginning of the correspondence he asked his young friend a probing question, "Who tells you who you are?" As chaplain at Yale for a number of years, he knew full well the power of higher education to tell students who they are.[1]

There are powerful forces in our culture that impact and shape who we think we are. The Christian answer I was given as a young person is that we are all sinners. Certainly that is true. I know that I am flawed and fail regularly to live up to the best ideals of humanity, or even my own best ideals. All of us are a mass of contradictions. But is that the first and foremost thing about us?

This is not what compassionate parents teach their children—at least, not at first. We tell them how special they are, how much they are loved and cared for, and what possibilities they have.

I find it interesting in Paul's letter to the Romans that before Paul expounds on the human problem, he identifies his readers as those who are loved by God, who belong to Jesus Christ, and who are, by divine call, saints (1:6-7). Most of us tend to think that a saint is someone particularly holy, set apart from the rest of us, someone who has achieved something very special. But in Paul's view, all Christians are saints.

One aspect of faith involves saying "yes" to our sainthood. Faith is our acceptance of God's unconditional acceptance. We are first the daughters and sons of God before we are sinners. Toxic religion turns that around. Unhealthy religion teaches that we are first unworthy, under God's wrath, and must be saved from our sin. Healthy religion says that we are first secure in God's love, that we are saints already, called to live as God's beloved children daily.

Once we accept that we are accepted and experience being loved by the one who sustains all existence, we then find the sacred space and inner courage to face the tensions and contradictions that our sin creates. When we know we are loved by the divine lover, we find the confidence and inner strength to confront our false self (our little ego-driven self with its propensity to grasp, grab, and cling to that which we think will bring ego satisfaction). Knowing that we are valued and have worth for simply being alive, we no longer feel the need to deny or repress our dark side. Our freedom to name our demons is the first step in overcoming them.

In the movie, *The Stand* (a classic tale of the conflict between good and evil based on Stephen King's book), an African-American woman known as Mother Abigail was depicted as the Christ figure. One of her inner disciples was a deaf mute. He was a man of great compassion and integrity, but he didn't believe in God.

In one scene, Mother Abigail talked about the role this young man would play in accomplishing God's will. His friend interjected, "But he doesn't believe in God." Not the least bit surprised or shaken, Mother Abigail turned gently and communicated directly to the young deaf man: "That's okay child, because God believes in you."

It's true. In spite of all our mishaps and foibles, all the ways we become entrapped and addicted that diminished our lives and relationships, God still believes in us. If enough of us really believed that, our world could be transformed. We are first and foremost saints, before we are sinners.

Going Deeper

1. What do you think about the idea that we are saints before we are sinners, that the first and best thing about each of us is that we are children of God?

2. How can "accepting that we are accepted as we are" help bring about positive change in our lives and relationships?

3. Would it make a difference in your life today if you could believe in the core of your being that God believes in you? How might that change your attitudes and outlook?

4. In his book, *Life of the Beloved*, Henri Nouwen wrote: "Self-rejection is the greatest enemy of the spiritual life because it contradicts the sacred voice that calls us the 'Beloved.' Being the Beloved expresses the core truth of our existence."[2] How might acceptance of this "core truth" give us stability and inner strength when we become victims of our cruel world?

When the Old-Time Religion No Longer Works

In the little book of Habakkuk, the prophet faces a crisis of faith. It is a common belief among Habakkuk's people that plagues and invasions from other nations are indicative of God's displeasure or judgment. Undoubtedly, Habakkuk shares this belief to some degree. Most of us share the beliefs we are socialized into through family and culture.

The Babylonians are coming. They are a ruthless and violent people who worship might and power. They will sweep down and set their hooks and nets into the land and gather the people of Israel in like a fisherman gathers in his catch, to be used and disposed of at will (1:5-17).

The prophet cries to God, "We cry for help but you do not listen. We cry out for deliverance but you do not save. The wicked hem in the righteous so that justice is perverted" (1:2-4).

It's a question of justice. How can it be, cries the prophet, that God would use a more wicked people to punish a less wicked people? The people of Israel aren't innocent, but they are not as vicious and ruthless as the Chaldeans. This baffles the prophet and sends him into a quandary. The old theology, the standard answer, no longer works.

I heard about a man traveling on a dinner flight who found an enormous roach on his salad. Back home he wrote a harsh letter to the president of the airline. A few days later he received a letter from the president explaining how that particular airplane had been fumigated and all the seats and upholstery stripped. There was even the suggestion that the aircraft would be taken out of service. The man was very impressed until he noticed that quite by accident the letter he had written had stuck to the president's letter. On his letter there was a note that said, "Reply with the regular roach letter."

For more and more Christians today, especially critically-thinking Christians, the old answers, the generic responses, are no longer sufficient.

Unfortunately, there are still many Christian communities that try to smother the questions. Questions arise that either we are not encouraged to ask or perhaps not even allowed to ask. And when we do ask them, we are given short, simplistic explanations or the questions are dismissed or ignored as insignificant. Or even worse, we are condemned for our lack of faith or treated as heretics for asking them.

For many Christians in faith communities across the country there are teachings that dare not be challenged and questions that dare not be asked. The old answers are supposed to be true because someone in authority says they are true. The answers usually are passed on as: "This is what the Bible says."

If the answers come from people we love and care about—such as our parents, family members, faith community, and friends in our social network—we may live with those answers for a long time, until they no longer work or make sense to us.

Sometimes it takes an experience of unusual suffering or loss to jar us awake—the death of a loved one, the breakup of a marriage, the loss of employment, a debilitating disease. Or it may come about, as it did in my faith journey, through a growing feeling or gnawing sense that the old answers are simply not true, that the "old time religion" is not spiritually healthy or personally transforming.

At some point in our faith journey it is necessary to find our beliefs/ theology lacking. Otherwise, we would never question and grow. Healthy, holistic, and transformative spirituality is not about having the right answers; it's about asking the right questions—better questions.

Going Deeper

1. Are there any questions buried in the recesses of your soul that you have been afraid to ask? (Allow your spirit the freedom to run free. No question is off limits.)

2. Why do you think so many Christians seem to be fearful of and avoid the difficult questions of faith and life?

3. In his book *Falling Upward* Richard Rohr wrote, "The bottom line of the Gospel is that most of us have to hit some kind of bottom before we even start the real spiritual journey."[3] Why does it so often take an experience of pain or loss to awaken our conscience to the more profound questions and issues of life?

The Essence of an Inclusive Faith

Abraham Maslow contended that any adequate understanding of religious faith must take into consideration "peak experiences," or those experiences of existential communion with an ultimate reality that transcend the limited self.

Mystics who have had such experiences have reported that they felt a deep, expansive sense of belonging to every other person and to all creation, where they could see the beauty and goodness of all things. The mystics of various religious traditions call this reality different names: God, the Really Real, the Presence, Cosmic Christ, Spirit, Source of Life, Ultimate Reality, Ground of Being, the Divine, the Mystery, and so on.

The beliefs we draw upon to describe the experience and the names we use to identify the divine reality who is the source of the experience will always be inadequate. A living faith is the means by which we connect, commune, and cooperate with the divine Spirit that is within every human (we are all made in God's image) and that pervades and permeates all creation. Our beliefs are merely pointers; our human way of trying to grasp and explain what is beyond our comprehension.

Genuine mystical encounters always move the individual or community toward a more inclusive worldview and acceptance. The mystics tell us that whenever we respond in love, whenever we share our resources with those in need, whenever we forgive and show mercy and stand with the downtrodden, we step into the flow of the divine life.

I can't think of anything more urgently needed today than this sense of mutual belonging with all humankind and with all creation. There are many religions and belief systems, because the unfathomable mystery at the heart of life itself is beyond our understanding. Beliefs tend to divide us, but a living faith that enables us to experience the unconditional love that is gently guiding the universe in a non-coercive way has the power to unite us.

We might think of it this way: We are all on the river in a boat, the river being the flow of the Spirit "in whom we live and move and have our being" (Acts 17:28). There are many different kinds of boats in which to navigate the river, and we are all in some kind of boat. The boat represents our belief system, our worldview, the way we see God and the world and our relationship to both. We all (even atheists) have some sort of belief system.

Some of us are navigating the river well. Others of us are bouncing off rocks, getting stuck in the mud, or running aground. Still others are fighting the river, trying to go against the flow. And then there are many who are asleep in their boats; they are not consciously aware that they are in a boat on the river.

At the heart of an inclusive Christian gospel is the deep conviction that all creation is God's household and we are all God's children. The Spirit (the living, cosmic Christ) resides in each one of us. We are all being carried by the river.

When our belief system is healthy, we are able to flow with the river. Our beliefs will help inspire, sustain, and grow a living faith (a dynamic trust) that keeps us in conscious communion and cooperation with God's redemptive presence. I say "conscious" because we all are connected, we all are in the river, though many of us are not aware or awake to God's redemptive presence.

When our belief system is unhealthy and toxic—fear-based, arrogant, and rooted in hate or prejudice—it will stifle, hinder, and impede a living faith. It will keep us spiritually stagnant, and perhaps make us spiritually repugnant to fair-minded people.

I long for the day when more Christians will embrace an inclusive gospel, for when that happens we will spend less time attempting to convert people to our way of thinking/believing and trying to get them to join our "chosen" group. We will spend more time seeking peace, pursuing justice for the most vulnerable, practicing forgiveness, taking care of creation, and humbly serving one another.

Going Deeper

1. What is the connection between belief and mystical experience of the divine? Have you ever had an experience where you felt a spiritual connection or kinship with everyone and everything?

2. Thomas Merton wrote about a mystical experience he had: "Yesterday, in Louisville, at the corner of Fourth and Walnut, [I] suddenly realized that I loved all the people and that none of them were or could be totally alien to me . . . Thank God! Thank God! I am only another member of the human race, like the rest of them. I have the immense joy of being a man, a member of a race in which God Himself became incarnate. . . . And if only everybody could realize this! But it cannot be explained. There is no way of telling people that they are all walking around shining like the sun."[4] Spiritual writers describe this kind of experience as grace, a pure gift that cannot be earned. Is there anything we can do to prepare our souls to receive such a gift? What might that be?

3. Drawing upon the imagery of being on the divine river in a boat, how would you describe the way you are navigating the river? What can you do to ensure that you flow with the river?

4. According to the writer of 1 John, to abide in love is to abide in God. He says that "if we love one another, God lives in us, and his love is perfected in us" (4:12). Read 1 John 4:7-21. What characteristics of love does the writer emphasize? Is every experience of authentic love an experience of God?

Faithfulness Is More Important Than Veneration

I believe that the living Christ is far more interested in our commitment to God's covenant than our veneration of Christ's deity—a covenant that calls us to love God with the totality of our being and to love our neighbor (that includes the "enemy") as ourselves (see Luke 10:25-37). Jesus never encourages his disciples to exalt him; he calls them to follow him, to be his apprentices, to learn from him how to live in and for God's kingdom, to live humbly, trusting *Abba* (the loving Father/Mother), and to embrace his passion for the excluded, marginalized, and downtrodden.

At one time I had such an exalted view of Jesus and his divine status that it did me no earthly good. I could not touch or reach Jesus, because Jesus was so high and lifted up. I imagined Jesus as someone who never demonstrated a cultural bias or acted in a selfish way or entertained a single, lustful thought. He commanded the elements of nature, even walking on water. I knew I couldn't walk on water. So I worshiped and venerated Jesus, but I couldn't imagine being like Jesus.

That started to change when I read two books that were part of a doctoral seminar[5]: *Jesus Christ, Liberator,* written by liberation theologian Leonardo Boff, and *Jesus Within Judaism,* written by James Charlesworth, a New Testament scholar specializing in Christian origins. Then, a few years later, I read a book by Marcus Borg titled, *Meeting Jesus Again for the First Time.*

I was drawn to and captivated by the Jewish Jesus; Jesus as "the Son of Man"—the human one. As I began to understand Jesus in his culture—as a sage, a teacher of nonconventional and alternative wisdom, a prophet who subverted the system, a Spirit-immersed person driven by a vision of God's new world and moved by a deep compassion, especially for the poor, impoverished, and marginalized—I began to find Jesus appealing, a captivating force drawing me toward him.

No longer did I see Jesus as one so perfect or sinless he could not possibly be emulated, but as a human completely dedicated to the cause of God's kingdom and given to the good and well-being of others. No longer did I see Jesus as one who could walk on water, but as a deeply spiritual person devoted to healing the sick, loving the unlovable, caring for the diseased and demonized, challenging and confronting the injustice of the religious establishment, and exuding a contagious faith, hope, and love. I began to cultivate an understanding and vision of Jesus that was compelling, calling forth my best effort, challenging me to nurture the transformative virtues of moral courage, forgiveness, and compassion.

As I studied the Gospels, I was startled that Jesus never appears concerned about or centered on his own veneration or exaltation. In fact, when the persons he heals want to proclaim him as the Messiah, he tells them not to tell anyone. He tells his disciples that the people of the world seek positions of power, authority, and veneration, but it is not to be so with them. He instructs them to be servants of all, for the Son of Man did not come to be served, but to serve, and to give his life for the liberation of many (Mark 10:35-45).

It is Jesus' human vision of God's kingdom—the dream of a world made right through forgiveness and reconciliation, through distributive and restorative justice (where all have enough to live a flourishing life), through radical sharing and grace—that convicts and humbles me, and is slowly changing me (slowly, because old habits and entrenched attitudes do not die easily and I have a long way to go).

Going Deeper

1. Do you accept the basic thesis of this reflection that the living Christ is more interested in our loyalty to God's covenant than our veneration and worship? Why or why not? If the living Christ is as humble and self-giving as he is portrayed in the Gospels, why would he want to be worshiped?

2. In the above piece I explain that at one time my exalted, heavenly view of Jesus did me no earthly good. Have you ever had a similar experience of feeling so disconnected to the divine Christ that he was beyond your reach?

3. In what ways can the worship of the exalted Christ distract and divert our attention away from the actual life Jesus lived and his call to discipleship?

Openness to a Larger Vision

In *The Last Battle*, the final volume of *The Chronicles of Narnia*, C. S. Lewis described a delightful scene toward the end of the story. A group of dwarfs sit huddled together in a tight little knot thinking they are in a pitch black, smelly hole of a stable when in reality they are out in the midst of an endless, grassy green countryside with sun shining and blue sky overhead. Lucy, the most tenderhearted of the Narnian children, felt compassion for them. She tried to reason with them. Then frustrated, she cried, "It isn't dark, you poor stupid Dwarfs. Can't you see? Look up! Look round! Can't you see the sky and the trees and the flowers!"[6] But all they saw was pitch-black darkness.

      Aslan, the Christ figure, was present with them, but they weren't able to see him. When Aslan offered them the finest food, they thought they were eating spoiled meat scraps and sour turnips. Then when Aslan offered them the choicest wine, they mistook it for ditch water.

      How did the dwarfs become so blind? They had refused to join the Narnians in their battle against evil. But they didn't actually join the other side either. Their one constant refrain was: the dwarfs are for the dwarfs. They lived by that mantra.

      That, I think, could pass for the philosophy of our age. We tend to live for "me" and "mine"—our family, our group, our tribe, our party, our nation. This pervades our politics, economics, religion, and all dimensions of society. Many politicians don't even try to conceal their true motives these days. They just state openly that their number-one goal is to defeat the other side. There is little interest in the common good and almost no interest in empowering the disadvantaged.

Many highly popular Christian leaders in our nation talk primarily about self-fulfillment, the keys to success (American style) and living a happy life, or the joys of the afterlife. This is why it is so remarkable today when someone actually breaks away from party lines to say or do what he or she thinks is right for the common good and what is morally just and compassionate. It's remarkable because it's so rare. And it usually means vocational suicide.

In John 1, Philip tells Nathaniel he has discovered Israel's Messiah—Jesus of Nazareth, son of Joseph. Nathaniel remarks, "Can anything good come out of a despised little town like Nazareth?" I'm sure Nathaniel's prejudice against Nazareth was part of his upbringing and heritage. Philip does not argue, but says, "Come and see." Take an honest look. Remarkably, Nathaniel is open, honest, and receptive enough to set aside his bias and discover the truth (see vv. 43-51).

I wonder how many of us are blind to truth and do not actually know God (though we may think we do), because we are unwilling to question our biases and assumptions. I wonder how often we miss what God is doing, because we keep chanting the mantra of our particular group or tribe, unwilling to consider how God may be at work in other communities and faith traditions.

Can we become humble, open, honest, and receptive enough to see the larger picture of God's dream for the world? Can we admit that God is much greater than what our little minds can capture and vastly more expansive than what our singular creeds and confessions expound (as important as these may be to our own faith)? Can we acknowledge that God's love is immensely deeper and wider than we can experience or even imagine? Our capacity today to respond to the Spirit and participate in God's work is vitally connected to our humility and openness to a larger vision of what God is doing in the world.

Going Deeper

1. It is possible to experience life through connection to three stories: my story, our story, and God's story. God's story is what Jesus called the kingdom of God. In what ways do we get stuck in the first two stories, preventing us from seeing and participating in God's story? How can our individual egos and group loyalties blind us from seeing God's larger vision?

2. According to Matthew 6:25-34, how important is it to give priority to the kingdom of God and God's restorative and distributive justice? (Clarence Jordan called this "the God Movement.") How can engagement with the larger vision of God's story help free us from our personal addictions and group idolatries?

3. Compare the Lord's Prayer in Matthew 6:9-13 with the once highly popular prayer of Jabez in 1 Chronicles 4:9-10. What "stories" are emphasized? How might we explain the popularity of the prayer of Jabez among American Christians?

Discovering a Living Faith

There can be a vast difference between a living faith and adherence to a system of religious beliefs. In the Gospels, faith has nothing to do with doctrinal beliefs about Jesus and everything to do with trust in Jesus as a mediator of God's grace and love.

For example, in one Gospel story a woman, suffering with a chronic bleeding condition that renders her unclean according to Jewish law, believes that if she could just touch Jesus' clothing she would be healed. Her belief reflects a popular cultural myth claiming that the powers of a healer (there were other healers in the ancient world besides Jesus) extended to the healer's clothes.

When she touches the garment of Jesus, healing power goes out to her, without Jesus intending it. Jesus says to the woman, "Your faith has made you whole" (see Mark 5:25-34). There is no intimation in the biblical account that she believed Jesus to be the Messiah or anything like what later Christians mean when they ascribe to Jesus the title, "Son of God."

In this story, faith constitutes a simple, humble, and risky act of trust in Jesus as the mediator of the healing power of God. The woman risks the hostility of the religious authorities because everyone she touches in the crowd she renders unclean according to Jewish purity law.

A living faith awakens us to God's presence, sensitizes us to God's movements, and connects us to the renewing, healing grace, forgiveness, and mercy of God. It is not some propositional or dogmatic belief about Jesus; it is, rather, a child-like trust, humility, and vulnerability that opens the disciple up to the dynamic presence of the living Christ.

Years ago I thought that what one believed about Jesus was what changed a person. I was wrong. The evidence is fairly conclusive. Some of the most doctrinally certain Christians can be the most difficult to get along with. Confident in their beliefs "about" Jesus, they lack the love, grace, and humility "of" Jesus.

A Christian belief is what we think and endorse about some aspect of Christian teaching (God, Jesus, the Bible, etc.) at a particular stage on our faith journey. As we grow in love and grace, our beliefs change. If our beliefs never change, there is a high probability that we are stagnant and not growing spiritually. I have discarded many of the beliefs I once held, but my faith is stronger today than ever before.

I am not suggesting that faith is devoid of all belief or intellectual content. There is something to be said for a reasonable faith, as opposed to a blind faith or one that lacks intellectual credibility. But faith does not deal in certainties and reason alone does not open us up to God. Certitude is usually rooted in fear, which explains why some people become so defensive about their beliefs.

"We see through a glass dimly," says Paul in his great exposition of love in 1 Corinthians 13. There's no infallible experience of God: no inerrant Bible or infallible tradition or perfect anything. But we can and do experience love, and love is foundational and essential to the nature of divine reality.

A living faith nurtures an awareness of and receptivity to the divine love that pervades the universe—a love that Christians believe became incarnate in Jesus of Nazareth.

Intellectual assent or doctrinal belief in God, Jesus, the Bible, heaven, salvation, or anything else does little, in and of itself, to change us. It is our experience of divine love that frees us from our ego, opens us up to the mystery, and is transformative in our lives and relationships.

Going Deeper

1. What are the differences between having a faith "about" Jesus and having the faith "of" Jesus? How would you describe the faith of Jesus?

2. In his classic, *Jesus Before Christianity*, Albert Nolan, wrote: "Faith was an attitude that people caught from Jesus through their contact with him, almost as if it were a kind of infection. It could not be taught, it could only be caught. And so they begin to look to him to increase their faith (Luke 17:5) or to help their unbelief (Mark 9:24). Jesus was the initiator of faith. But once it had been initiated it could spread from one person to another. The faith of one person could awaken faith in another. The disciples were sent out to awaken faith in others."[7] How might we awaken faith in one another and in the people we know and meet outside our faith communities?

3. In John 15:1-17, abiding in Christ is equivalent to abiding in love. What part does a "living faith" play in nurturing a life of love, a kind of life that produces "much fruit"? What does this "fruit" consist of and look like? How can a living faith, which results quite naturally in a flourishing life, be cultivated and developed?

4. What kind of "power" is the prayer in Ephesians 3:14-21 talking about? What does it mean for Christ to dwell in our hearts through faith and to be filled with the fullness of God?

Taste and See That God Is Good

A living faith enables us, in the words of the psalmist, to "taste and see" the goodness of God (Ps. 34:8). It gives us the capacity to intuit God's presence in the world and in our lives. The more we nurture this capacity to "taste and see" God's goodness in the events and experiences of our lives, the more we are able to see God everywhere.

Even if you are not a baseball fan, you may have heard about the blown call by umpire Jim Joyce during the 2010 season that prevented Detroit pitcher Armando Galarraga from pitching a perfect game (an accomplishment that has occurred only twenty times in the 141-year history of Major League baseball).

With only one batter left to face, Joyce called a runner safe at first, when in reality (as instant replay conclusively demonstrated) he was out by half a step. This made quite a splash in the media, but in my estimation the real story took place afterward.

Galarraga couldn't believe the call; he knew the batter was out. He knew the implications of what just took place. Yet, he was calm—no emotional outburst, no blame (he left that for the manager), just a smile and back to work to finish his job. Galarraga's restraint was truly an exercise of grace.

After the game when umpire Joyce watched the replay and realized he had blown the call, he was sick with remorse. Refusing to hide his emotion, he publicly admitted he was wrong and expressed a gut-wrenching personal apology to Galarraga and baseball fans everywhere, offering no excuses.

But perhaps the most striking and moving scene took place the following day when Joyce, as scheduled, assumed his duties as home plate umpire for the next game in the series. Each team is responsible for bringing the starting lineup to the umpire behind the plate. Usually this is the task of the manager or a coach or a team captain, but this day it was Galarraga himself who walked out of the Detroit dugout. Galarraga and Joyce met in full view of a stadium of people and shook hands. Joyce was so emotional he couldn't speak. With eyes full of tears and lips trembling, he accepted the lineup card and gently touched Galarraga on the arm.

Forgiveness was extended and accepted; mercy was given and received. Some fans did not appreciate the gesture. Some cheered. It was a moment of grace, and in the world of professional competitive baseball, extravagant grace, even scandalous grace.

One Christian writer describing this encounter between Galarraga and Joyce said that he experienced the event as a "thin place," a phrase that emerged with Celtic Christianity in the fifth century. A "thin place" is a place where the world of God and the world of creation touch, a place where God's radiant goodness becomes palpable, a place where the veil is pulled back a bit and we are able to see a little more clearly the grace and love present in life.

God is with all of us, but not all of us are aware of God's presence. God's grace abounds, but not all of us taste and see God's goodness. A living faith gives us a consciousness and an imagination for grasping this experience. It gives us a language, a vocabulary, to talk about it and express our gratitude.

A living faith has little or nothing to do with certitudes, dogma, or doctrinal statements about God that we can check off as true or false. It has everything to do with tasting and seeing the grace and goodness in life that point to God's presence among us and within us.

Going Deeper

1. In *The Heart of Christianity*, Marcus Borg wrote: "Thin places are places where the veil momentarily lifts and we behold God . . . A thin place is anywhere our hearts are opened . . . a means whereby the sacred becomes present to us."[8] While these experiences are received as grace, and not based on any system of meritocracy, what spiritual practices might we engage in that would help make our spirits and souls more ready to encounter "thin places"?

2. In Genesis 28:10-17, Jacob has an experience where the veil is lifted and he encounters God. It comes to him in a dream. He exclaims, "Surely the Lord is in this place—and I did not know it" . . . This is none other than the house of God, and this is the gate of heaven." Can you describe an experience that became a "gate of heaven" for you?

3. Our capacity to experience "thin places" is often related to the condition of our hearts and minds, whether they are open or closed, receptive or distracted, tuned in or tuned out. What factors and elements come into play in determining the condition of our hearts and minds? What factors are within your power to change, and what factors are beyond your control? When do you know that your heart is open or closed? What characteristics mark a closed or open heart?

Notes

[1]William Sloan Coffin, *Letters to a Young Doubter* (Louisville: WJK, 2005), 5-9.

[2]Henri J. M. Nouwen, *Life of the Beloved: Spiritual Living in a Secular World* (New York: Crossroad Publishing Co., 1992), 33.

[3]Richard Rohr, *Falling Upward: A Spirituality for the Two Halves of Life* (San Francisco: Jossey-Bass, 2011), 138.

[4]Thomas Merton, *A Year with Thomas Merton: Daily Meditations from His Journals*, ed. Jonathan Montaldo (New York: HarperSanFrancisco, 2004), 81.

[5]This was at Southern Baptist Seminary in 1991, just before the fundamentalist takeover of the seminary and the mass exodus of progressively oriented professors.

[6]C. S. Lewis, *The Chronicles of Narnia*, 1st American ed. (New York: HarperCollins, 2001), 746.

[7]Albert Nolan, *Jesus Before Christianity*, 25th anniv. ed. (Maryknoll, NY: Orbis Books, 2002), 40.

[8]Marcus J. Borg, *The Heart of Christianity: How We Can Be Passionate Believers Today* (New York: HarperSanFrancisco, 2003), 156.

CHAPTER 3

A New Way for a New Day
(Christianity)

Christianity Is a Way of Life

Biblical scholar Marcus Borg wrote about sitting next to a passenger on a plane who told him, "I'm much more interested in Buddhism and Sufism than I am in Christianity." When Borg asked why, she said, "Because they're about a way of life, and Christianity is all about believing."[1]

Unfortunately, this is the way Christianity is often perceived. Ask a friend what he or she thinks is meant by the phrase "true believer" and most likely your friend will say something about having correct beliefs. What one believes about God, Jesus, and other teachings of the Christian faith, however, is only one aspect of Christian faith.

Borg noted that this is a rather odd notion when you think about it—that God would care that much about the beliefs we have in our heads, as if believing the right things is what God is after. It seems more likely that God would be interested in the way we actually live—how we love and care for one another and our planet—than the limited, flawed, inaccurate beliefs we cling to in our minds.

It is not just progressive Christians who make this point. Evangelical philosopher and theologian Dallas Willard, in his book, *The Divine Conspiracy*, has spoken disparagingly of what he calls "bar code faith."

Think of the bar codes on products we purchase. The scanner responds only to the bar code. It makes no difference what is actually in the package, bottle, or container. The scanner reads the bar code through its electronic eye and then assigns a value.

Many Christians conceive of salvation very similarly. They think that by believing certain things about Jesus—that he is divine, that he died for our sins and was raised from the dead, etc. (for some Christians it is a fairly long list)—God saves the believer (understood primarily as being forgiven and fit for heaven) and that is what constitutes a Christian.

Willard asked: "Can we seriously believe that God would establish a plan for us that essentially bypasses the awesome needs of present human life and leaves human character untouched? . . . Can we believe that the essence of Christian faith and salvation covers nothing but death and after? Can we believe that being saved really has nothing whatever to do with the kinds of persons we are?"[2]

There are reasons, some simple and some complex, why this understanding of Christian salvation developed, but it certainly did not originate with Jesus of Nazareth as he is portrayed in the Gospels. According to Jesus, participation in the kingdom of God involves a lifestyle of nonviolence, forgiveness, compassion, peacemaking, reconciliation, and the pursuit of restorative (redemptive) and distributive (where everyone has enough of this world's resources to live a flourishing life) justice.

This is why, in the book of Acts, Christians are designated as those who "belong to the way" (9:2)—not the way to heaven. Jesus rarely spoke of heaven. Rather he proclaimed and incarnated the compassionate power of the kingdom of God and told his followers to pray for its realization on earth.

What one believes about Jesus is not nearly as important as the daily commitment to be like Jesus. A head belief is useless, unless it is able to transform the heart, so that "the believer" exudes the faith, hope, and love of Jesus and aspires to pursue his compassionate, nonviolent, self-giving way of life.

Going Deeper

1. Dallas Willard has noted that many Christians "have been led to believe that God for some unfathomable reason, just thinks it appropriate to transfer credit from Christ's merit account to ours, and to wipe out our sin debt, upon inspecting our mind and finding that we believe a particular theory of the atonement to be true—even if we trust everything but God in all other matters that concern us."[3] Why do you think this approach to faith (having correct beliefs) has become so popular in American Christianity?

2. What are the major differences in trusting some arrangement God has made for sin remission through Jesus and trusting the living presence of Christ in order to live according to his teachings and pattern of life?

3. In what ways can a growing and deepening trust in the real presence and redemptive power of the living Christ transform the way we see and experience life?

Toxic Christianity

The Shawshank Redemption is at the top of my all-time great movies list. It is peppered with great lines and immersed in a rich spiritual symbolism. The warden, Samuel Norton, is an icon of toxic Christianity. When Andy and the other prisoners made their first appearance before the warden, his self-righteousness dominated the scene. He had one of the prisoners beaten for asking, "When do we eat?" Holding forth a Bible, he told the prisoners, "Trust in the Lord, but your ass is mine."

The warden presented himself as a socially respectable, church-going, Bible-quoting Christian. But it's clear from the moment he appeared in the story that his Christianity was in name only. In one scene, the warden entered Andy's cell. He took Andy's Bible as Andy and the warden quoted Scripture verses back and forth. The warden did not open the Bible, which was good for Andy since the rock hammer he used to tunnel through the cell wall was hidden inside. When he handed the Bible back to Andy, he spoke truth beyond his knowledge: "Salvation lies within."

The final verse the warden quoted was John 8:12, "I am the light of the world. Whoever follows me will never walk in darkness but will have the light of life." Of course, the warden did not have the foggiest notion what that verse really meant. The warden walked in darkness and was about as blind and unliberated a person as you would ever find. But he thought he was a Christian.

Christianity (as well as toxic religion in general) can be as deadly and destructive as it can be redemptive and life-giving. Our wardrobe of Christian faith can become a cunningly disguised way of protecting the ego. I suppose we are all guilty of this to one degree or another.

Religion can become a clever way for us to feel secure, to feel superior (we are the ones chosen while the rest are passed over and excluded), and to be in control. Jesus, in the Gospels, sees right through this. Isn't it interesting that he finds hospitable table fellowship, not with the moral majority, but with the immoral minority? Those who think they can see are actually blind, while those who know they are blind find spiritual sight (read John 9).

Authentic spirituality is not about being correct or citing Bible passages. It's not about wearing the right badges or shouting the right pledges. It's about being humble enough to admit that we are blind, so that the divine Spirit can lead us to a place where we can see.

There is no magic formula: Believe this, do this, practice this. There are no four spiritual laws, five steps, six principles, or seven habits for highly spiritual people. But somehow our illusions must be exposed and we must face the many ways we both protect and parade our egos. Somehow we must surrender to a greater love and greater story, instead of being so absorbed in our own little stories where we are so easily offended and hurt and become bitter, jealous, and resentful people. Somehow we must let go of our need for power, position, prestige, and possessions that dominates Western life, and become more passionate about what Jesus called the kingdom of God.

I wish I could offer you a prescription, but there is none, other than following Jesus. Transformative spiritual persons are fairly easy to detect, though. You can see the love and compassion in their eyes, their face, their words and gestures. Their whole body radiates the light of Christ. They are gentle, understanding, humble, empathetic, and yet, at the same time, they can be bold, courageous, and unafraid to challenge the powers that be.

Why are there so few transformed people and communities/churches in Western/American Christianity? Could it be that our toxic versions of Christian faith have become not only all too common but also the standard?

Going Deeper

1. What are some ways we use our Christian faith to protect, defend, and assert our egos? Why is it so hard for us recognize when our faith becomes toxic?

2. Read the story in John 9:1-41. What does Jesus mean when he says that he has come to render a proper "judgment" or discernment "so that those who do not see may see, and those who do see may become blind?" (9:39). What might we do to help the Spirit break through our ego defenses and layers of protection so that we might "see" with more clarity what is true and real?

3. Spend a few moments in silence asking God to open your heart so that you might honestly and humbly see "what is." Then consider the following question: In what ways is my Christian faith toxic and diminishing, and in what ways is it healthy and transformative?

Let the Church Be the Church

Author Ann Rice opened her heart to God in 1998, returning to her faith after years of describing herself as an atheist. She explained her journey away from faith and back again in her 2008 memoir, *Called Out of Darkness: A Spiritual Confession.*

In August of 2010, she decided to leave Christianity, renouncing her claim to be "Christian," though she has not renounced her claim to be a follower of Christ. She wrote on her Facebook page:

> For those who care, and I understand if you don't: Today I quit being a Christian. I'm out. I remain committed to Christ as always but not to being "Christian" or to being part of Christianity. It's simply impossible for me to "belong" to this quarrelsome, hostile, disputatious, and deservedly infamous group. For ten years, I've tried. I've failed. I'm an outsider. My conscience will allow nothing else.

As a Christian minister and pastor, I cannot acquiesce to Rice's departure, but I certainly understand it. Too often institutional Christianity (both conservative and liberal) reflects very little of the Christ we encounter in the Gospels who befriends sinners and outcasts, challenges the status quo, and champions the cause of the poor and oppressed.

There are some observers of the religious landscape who believe that we are entering a new era in the evolution of Christian faith. There are churches and faith communities that are becoming less preoccupied with creedal conformity and more passionate about actually walking in the way of Jesus. They are becoming less institutional and ensconced within an antique shop of dusty beliefs, and more engaged in the work of God's kingdom on earth.

I am hopeful that the Constantinian age of Christianity, with its insistence on doctrinal correctness, patriarchal structure, and its unhealthy focus on the afterlife and "hell evasion," is beginning to give way to a new era of dynamic, inclusive, compassionate Christianity that is committed to peacemaking, equality and justice for all, and visible, specific, tangible expressions of God's unconditional love.

There will be resistance. Change will not come without backlashes and setbacks. The religious powers are committed to maintaining the status quo and protecting their own interests. There will be those on the theological right who will dig in and circle their wagons. There will be those on the theological left who will remain indifferent and apathetic. But despite opposition and apathy, new ways are emerging.

Churches serving as outposts for the God movement on earth will be more flexible in both theology and structure. They will hold many of their beliefs tentatively, while nurturing a deep, living faith in the goodness, grace, forgiveness, and unconditional love of God embodied in the life, teachings, death, and vindication/resurrection of Jesus.

They will affirm the identity of all people as God's beloved children. They will be more ecologically minded and committed to cultivating a healthy, life-affirming relationship with all creation. They will be given to growing loving relationships, not only within their own family and friend networks and churches, but also with persons of other faiths and persons with no faith at all without feeling the need to convert them to their way of thinking or believing.

My word to Christians on the verge of leaving the church: Don't abandon ship. We need you. The Spirit of the living, cosmic Christ is at work in our world, and yes, even in the institutional church—shattering illusions, opening minds and hearts, inspiring suffering love, and ever drawing us into a new stage of Christ consciousness and compassionate community.

Going Deeper

1. Do you think a Christian is ever justified in abandoning the church? Why or why not?

2. What are the negatives and positives of institutional Christianity? Do you think being part of a faith community is essential to living out one's discipleship to Christ? Why or why not?

3. Former Harvard Professor Harvey Cox has argued that, historically, Christianity is moving into the Age of the Spirit where "the spiritual, communal, and justice-seeking dimensions of Christianity are now its leading edge" and a growing number of Christians "are more interested in ethical guidelines and spiritual disciplines than in doctrines."[4] Do you agree with Cox's assessment? In your estimation, what would the ideal Christian community look like? What new forms of church can you imagine?

Christianity Must Lose Its Dualism

At a national gathering of Christians in 2010, a theme reiterated throughout the meeting was the "lostness" of the world. One leader said, "We need to be looking forward with an aggressive agenda to penetrate lostness around the world and in North America." Another leader said, "Every pastor has to walk away from this convention asking, 'What can I do . . . to make a difference by penetrating lostness?'" Still another popular spokesperson proclaimed, "I think God has put in the forefront in all our minds the tremendous lostness not only of the world . . . but also of North America. We are a nation of lostness." The reporter who quoted these leaders assessed the theme of the meeting as "a fresh look at the lostness of our nation and world."

Of course, none of the leaders or those in their group would consider the possibility that the "lostness" they were talking about could possibly include themselves. It's always the "other" people who are lost. Until there is fundamental change in the theology, God-image, and basic worldview that undergird all this talk of lostness, I can't see how such dualistic versions of Christianity will offer any hope to our world.

As membership within American churches declines, the solution for those committed to either/or thinking seems to be louder rhetoric (shout louder) and more aggressive strategies (work harder) to proselytize those they believe are lost.

At one time I believed that I was one of God's elect, God's chosen, and everyone else who didn't share my faith in Jesus was "lost," "unsaved," or "under the wrath of God." Though it pains me now to admit this, I even used words and phrases such as "doomed" and "condemned" and "children of the devil" to describe all those who did not fit my definition of a Christian.

I have a notion that wherever such dualistic versions of Christianity prevail, Christianity will increasingly become irrelevant, and will, most likely, become more of a hindrance than a help in healing and bettering our world. Dualistic religion tends to polarize and divide, establishing the "in" group (the chosen, the ones who alone possess the truth, etc.) as superior.

This trend will become more evident in major urban centers than in small, conservative towns, but eventually even the most Christian-entrenched areas will feel the impact. This diminished interest in dualistic Christianity is now widespread in Europe, and America is not far behind.

According to recent surveys and studies, only about 10 to 20 percent of America's younger generation are finding a connection to Christian faith. Most church growth comes at the expense of membership loss from other churches. Megachurches are in some sense both the result of and cause of this loss in smaller churches. All signs point toward decreased interest in Christianity, even among those who claim to be Christians. From the perspective of dualistic Christianity, it is more difficult these days to get "lost" people "saved," and more of the "saved" are rejecting the faith once embraced.

I am convinced that traditional Christianity has to change (in both its conservative and liberal forms) in order to be a positive, redemptive influence in our world. And what must change are not only the methods we use to proclaim the Christian faith, but also the very Christian message we proclaim. Our basic understanding of God and God's relationship to the world through Christ must become more inclusive, holistic, compassionate, ecological, and reconciliatory or Christianity will increasingly be regarded with both indifference and disdain. Some secular visions of a global community are much more holistic and redemptive than many Christian dualistic visions (for example, the whole "Left Behind" scenario). It would seem that the spiritual consciousness of some secularists is more evolved and developed than the spiritual consciousness of many Christians embracing "us" versus "them" versions of faith.

The sad and ironic thing about all of this is that the good news of Jesus— the inclusive message he proclaimed and the compassionate life he lived—is often lost to the very ones who herald him as Savior.

Going Deeper

1. The Bible contains a lot of dualistic language. Insider and outsider language is a common feature of apocalyptic worldviews that emerge in times of great oppression. The New Testament developed out of an apocalyptic milieu pervasive in Palestinian Judaism during the time of Jesus. (I recommend reading the excellent article on apocalypticism in the *Anchor Bible Dictionary* by John Collins.) How might we interpret the dualistic language in the Bible without linking insider and outsider language to the will and purpose of God?

2. In many dualistic versions of Christian faith, the outsiders are excluded because their beliefs/doctrines are judged to be inaccurate and wrong. How could one possibly feel safe, secure, trustful, or loved by such a small, arbitrary God? Why do people cling to an image of God who excludes people for petty reasons?

3. Try interpreting dualistic Scriptures in more inclusive, holistic, and redemptive ways. Read Matthew 13:24-30. Instead of interpreting the "weeds" and the "wheat" as people groups, let them represent the good and evil, light and darkness, positive and negative qualities that reside in all of us.

Hope for the Evangelical Church

Author and former mega-church pastor Rob Bell made a huge splash in the Christian world with his book, *Love Wins: A Book About Heaven, Hell, and the Fate of Every Person Who Ever Lived.* Even though Bell has denied in numerous interviews that he embraces universalism, the vision of Christianity he expounds is close to what I would call "hopeful universalism." He argues against the traditional idea of hell and for the possibility of redemption after death.

As a progressive Christian, I am not completely satisfied with Bell's argument. I felt he needed a more consistent hermeneutic (method of interpretation) to deal with the many dualistic passages in the New Testament, which he mostly avoided. He also failed, in my judgment, to show the connection between God's triumph of love and the redemptive significance of Jesus' death. He clearly believes Jesus' death has saving efficacy, but he never theorizes how. These criticisms are minor, however, in light of the genuinely hopeful view he expounds.

Bell's basic Christian perspective is, of course, nothing new. But it is the first time, as far as I know, that a mega-church pastor, educated in and emerging from an evangelical tradition, has had the courage to publicly proclaim a more inclusive, holistic vision. A few other popular, influential Christian leaders are moving in that direction, but have not quite arrived there yet.

A case in point is Rick Warren, mega-church pastor and author of *The Purpose-Driven Life*. On one occasion Warren served on a panel with the late Peter Gomes, minister of Harvard University's Memorial Church and Plummer Professor of Christian Morals. The question was asked whether one could be saved who was not a born-again Christian. Gomes responded that he could not imagine that the God who created everything would have no other plan of salvation for the billions of other people in the world, or even beyond our galaxy, except the New Testament one. Warren, as reported by Gomes in his book, *The Scandalous Gospel of Jesus*, was as generous as his theology would allow, but could not, on the basis of John 14:6, concede the possibility that others might find salvation outside of Christ.[5]

This did not particularly strike me as noteworthy until I discovered in a book written by Rabbi David J. Wolpe, titled *Why Faith Matters*, that Warren had written the foreword. In it, Warren spoke highly of Wolpe as a man of faith and personal experience of God. He declared, "I'm certain that the profound insights in this book will stimulate your thinking and even touch your soul about the reality of God in fresh and surprising ways."[6]

The reason I find this all so intriguing is that, according to Warren's evangelical theology, Rabbi Wolpe has not been saved by Jesus Christ (in the way that Warren interprets John 14:6) and is, therefore, destined for hell. Wolpe has not been "born again," is not a Christian, and yet Warren commended Wolpe as a man who knows and speaks about "the reality of God in fresh and surprising ways.[6]

Here is an example of a highly popular evangelical leader who evidently does not yet see the contradiction he embraces, or else chooses to ignore it. In my estimation, it is an example of an evangelical leader who has emotionally, spiritually, and psychologically outgrown his dualistic, exclusivistic theology, but who does not yet have the courage to admit it, either to himself or his immense fan base.

Rob Bell gives me hope for the evangelical church. It is slow in coming, but there is an evolving spiritual consciousness that is touching all areas of religious life. Let us hope that it will one day lead to the kingdom of God on earth as envisioned by Jesus.

Going Deeper

1. How do you interpret Rick Warren's comment on Rabbi Wolpe? Do you think it is possible for Warren to defend his positive remarks in light of his dualistic theology?

2. Harvard religion professor Diana Eck told about being asked once by an elderly friend in India: "Do you really believe that God came only once, so very long ago and only to one people?" She said, "The very idea that God could be so stingy as to show up only once, to one people, in one part of the world exploded my understanding of incarnation."[7] How would you answer the question posed to Professor Eck?

3. As Christianity becomes more inclusive, more egalitarian, and more oriented around issues of restorative and distributive justice, it is inevitable that such gains will evoke an almost point-for-point fundamentalist response. What evidence do you see for the progressive movement and the fundamentalist reaction in Western Christianity today? In your own denomination, community, or church?

The Myth of Redemptive Violence

From the beginning of the post-Easter Jesus movement, disciples of Jesus have assigned redemptive significance to Jesus' death. A rich variety of metaphors are employed in the New Testament, particularly in Paul's letters, but never does Paul or any other writer attempt to offer a theological exposition or explanation of the metaphors employed. The metaphors are left loose and dangling and are subject to various interpretations.

Atonement theories that are prominent today can be grouped into two broad categories: Traditional Christianity is dominated by substitution/satisfaction theories, while these progressive Christians can be described as nonviolent participation (or moral influence) theories.

Substitution/satisfaction theories emphasize the necessity of Jesus' death for the forgiveness of sins. Within this framework, Jesus' death was required to satisfy God's offended justice or to appease/propitiate God's wrath. Jesus' death was demanded as a payment for the penalty of sin—a substitutionary sacrifice that bears the sinner's punishment. These theories view Jesus' violent death as a sacrifice demanded by God for the sinners' atonement.

Progressive Christians level numerous criticisms against any view of Jesus' death that seems to legitimize violence. Progressives suggest that some versions of substitutionary atonement reflect a picture of cosmic child abuse. Even Trinitarian formulations that emphasize the union between the Father and the Son must answer the question: Why does God need to save us from God?

Why would a God of love and grace demand a violent sacrifice in order to atone for sin? There is no system of justice apart from God. Why does God need to be paid off, or appeased, or have God's honor or justice satisfied before God can forgive? What does such a view say about the character of God? Jesus speaks of God as *Abba*, a loving parent who continually seeks what is best for God's children. God forgives because it is the nature of God to do so. God is a forgiving God.

This is what Jesus does in the Gospels. He forgives freely as God's agent of redemption (Matt. 9:1-6). According to Matthew's Gospel, this authority is given to all humans (9:7). Jesus welcomes all manner of sinners, accepting and forgiving them without requiring any sacrificial ritual or victim (9:9-13). In Matthew's version of the open table, Jesus even quotes Hosea: "I desire mercy, not sacrifice" (9:13).

In the Gospels, Jesus dies because he angers the religious establishment and the powers that be. He is a boundary breaker who violates and disregards purity laws that regulated holiness. He also constantly challenges the status quo by teaching an alternative wisdom and by proclaiming an alternative religious and social vision. And in the temple where the cultic sacrifices were offered, Jesus overturns the tables in protest against corrupt temple religion.

Progressive Christianity sees Jesus' death as a sacrifice of devotion to God's cause—he gives up his life while living for the good of others and doing the will of God. He puts the good of others and God's cause before his own life. But progressives do not believe that Jesus' death was necessary in order to make forgiveness of sins possible.

Perhaps the single word that best captures progressive interpretations of the redemptive value of Jesus' death is participation. Progressives contend that we are redeemed/transformed as we participate with Jesus in the way of the cross, the way of self-giving service, humility, nonviolence, forgiveness, and suffering love. Death and resurrection constitute the transformative pattern. As we die to our selfish attitudes and ambitions and center our lives in the Spirit, manifesting the grace and goodness of the Christ life, we participate in Christ's death and resurrection through the power of the Spirit (see Romans 6-8).

Jesus' death exposes the evil—the greed, hate, and violence—of the domination system. Jesus defeats the principalities and powers, not through violence but nonviolence, by bearing the animosity and cruelty inflicted upon him through patient endurance and forgiveness. Jesus absorbs the hate and violence of the powers without returning the hate and violence, thus making it possible for the cycle of hate and violence to be broken.

Progressives also see the death of Jesus as a powerful revelation of God's love for the world (Rom. 5:8). God's revelation of love in Christ inspires disciples of Jesus to offer their total selves to God as a living sacrifice, refusing to be conformed to the values of this world and embracing God's good and gracious will (Rom. 12:1-2). Jesus gave his life for God's cause, for a vision of a world healed and made whole. Through Jesus' life, death, resurrection, and continued presence his disciples are inspired and empowered to do likewise.

Traditional Christianity makes the sacrificial metaphors of Paul fit a substitution/satisfaction theory and then reads the Gospels through the grid of their interpretation of Paul. Progressive Christians give priority to the Gospels and either downplay the sacrificial metaphors of Paul or interpret them in nonsubstitutionary ways.

For example, when Paul says that Jesus "died for our sins" (1 Cor. 15:3) or "gave himself for our sins" (Gal. 1:4), progressives contend that such expressions can be interpreted in ways other than substitution. It may mean that Jesus died "on account of" or "because of" our sins—our sins being the sins of the domination system that crucified him. In other words, we are complicit in the system that crucified Jesus. Or it could mean that Jesus gave himself to deliver us from the controlling power of our sins like greed or hate. We are liberated from such sins as we follow Jesus in love of God and love of neighbor, even when our neighbor is the enemy who crucifies us.

It's very possible that Paul and other early Christians reference Jesus' death as a concise way of summarizing the whole Christ event—his incarnational life, death, resurrection/vindication, and continued presence through the Spirit. For example, in the Christ hymn of Philippians 2:6-11, Jesus' death is spoken of as the culmination of a life of humility, service, and obedience to the will of God.

Thus, progressive Christians see the cross of Jesus as a paradigm for radical transformation. As we follow the path of humility, sacrificial love, and surrender to God's will that culminated for Jesus in the cross, we are changed by the same Spirit that guided him. As we die to our small, ego-driven, false self, and live in the power of the Spirit, the power that generates suffering love and compassionate service, we conform to the way of the crucified Christ and grow in character and spiritual awareness. As we bear personal injustice through patient endurance and forgiveness, we clear a way forward for breaking the vicious cycles of hate and revenge, making reconciliation possible.

In substitution/satisfaction theories, salvation is often regarded as a kind of cosmic, legal, juridical transaction that, for all practical purposes, renders the life and teachings of Jesus irrelevant. In this system, forgiveness is basically a declaration of acquittal or pronouncement of "not guilty" in the heavenly courtroom based on Jesus bearing the penalty and paying the price for our sins. In nonviolent participation theories, forgiveness is understood in the way Jesus treats it in the Gospels. Jesus' concern is about restoring relationships, calling for repentance and reconciliation. For progressive Christians forgiveness is less a juridical pronouncement and more a relational process that constitutes a vital part of discipleship to Jesus.

Going Deeper

1. Progressive Christians contend that the nonviolent God of Jesus is incompatible with a God who makes a horrendous act of violence a divinely required act of atonement. What do you think?

2. If God required a violent sacrifice to atone for sin, would that justify our use of violence in dealing with evil? How could that be harmonized with the life and teaching of Jesus?

3. Progressive Christians argue that violence is never redemptive. It may at times curtail evil by force, but it cannot redeem evil. Progressive Christians argue that only forgiveness and love of enemy can break cycles of hate and violence, thus making redemption and reconciliation possible. What do you think?

Three Keys to Transformative Christianity

I believe there are at least three foundational characteristics of transformative Christianity. One is inclusiveness. Christianity that is unhealthy and toxic (and can be destructive and deadly) is always dualistic. It divides the world between "us" and "them." Obviously, in order to explain one's own faith or position, some differentiation and categorization is necessary, but this is vastly different than saying that only members of one's group or faith possess the truth or are accepted by God.

Inclusive Christianity does not believe that all roads lead to God or that all beliefs are equally valid. But it does contend that God will travel many different roads to get to us, and that truth is truth wherever it may be found.

The basic difference is this: Christians entrenched within exclusive Christianity insist that those outside their group must believe what they believe or relate to God the way they relate to God in order to become God's children. Inclusive Christianity begins with the core belief that all people are already children of God. It's all grace—radical, unconditional grace. It's not that some are chosen and others are not. We are all chosen.

For example, the best of the Hebrew tradition says that God chose Israel, not because God loved them more or because they were more special than others, but in order to communicate that "chosenness" to the rest of the world. So that through the seed of Abraham, all the peoples of the world would be blessed. This is at the heart of the Abrahamic covenant (see Gen. 12:1-3). It is also at the heart of inclusive Christian faith.

A second key characteristic of transformative Christianity is compassion. Compassion is both a feeling and a way of being that flows out of that feeling. In the English etymology, "passion" comes from the Latin word that means "to feel," and the prefix "com-" means "with." Compassion means "to feel with." To show compassion is to feel the hurt or pain of someone else and then, on the basis of that feeling, to act on that person's behalf. It includes the twin capacity to participate in both the suffering and the healing of someone else. Transformative Christianity looks to Jesus as the embodiment of what it means to be compassionate.

The third characteristic is conversion. Transformative Christianity results in real life change. Salvation is not merely about the afterlife, nor is it about some cosmic, judicial transaction that occurs when one believes certain things about Jesus. (Why would God care so much about specific beliefs anyway? None of our beliefs can capture the whole reality of God.)

Conversion is about becoming who we already are (children of God) and learning how to live as God's children in the world. It's about becoming persons and communities that exude integrity, humility, forgiveness, and compassion. It's about learning how to love—how to love one another in the church (the faith community) and those outside the church, accepting everyone as God's child and demonstrating God's kindness in how we treat and relate to others. In fact, the writer of 1 John argues that this is how we demonstrate our love for God, namely, by the way we love one another (see 1 John 3:11-20; 4:7-21).

Transformative Christianity is not about emotional worship services that leave everyone feeling good. It has nothing to do with how many religious activities the church offers, or how many people are attending, or how large the church budget is. It has nothing to do with American trappings of success. It has everything to do with how well we love, care for, serve, and uplift one another. Christians learn how to love through their discipleship to Jesus. Therefore, discipleship to Christ (being an apprentice of Christ) is at the very heart of the Christian gospel.

Going Deeper

1. What Richard Rohr has said about the first half of life can be said about many forms of institutional Christianity: It "is always about externals, formulas, superficial emotions, flags and badges, correct rituals, Bible quotes, and special clothing, all of which largely substitute for actual spirituality (see Matt. 23:13-32) . . . it is largely style and sentiment instead of real substance." He observed that "most people facing the transformative issues of social justice, divorce, failure, gender identity, an inner life of prayer, or any radical reading of the gospel are usually bored and limited by the typical Sunday church agenda."[8] What can a few people do within the institutional church to help bring about renewal?

2. Whereas beliefs and doctrines have been the first priority of institutional Christianity for many years now, religious commentator Dianna Butler Bass has argued that in transformational Christianity, believing takes a back seat to belonging and behaving. She wrote: "Relational community, intentional practice, and experiential belief are forming a new vision of what it means to be Christian . . . We belong to God and to one another, connected to all in a web of relationships, and there we find our truest selves. We behave in imitation of Jesus, practicing our faith with deliberation as we anticipate God's reign of justice and love. We believe with our entire being, trusting, beloving, and devoted to the God whom we have encountered through one another and in the world."[9] What can you do in your church and local Christian community to be an advocate for Christian faith that is dynamic and transformational and that promotes belonging and behaving over believing?

3. Are there ways to deconstruct the emphasis on beliefs and doctrines that have been so prevalent in Western Christianity so that we might reconstruct a faith that gives priority to inclusion, compassion, and conversion? What steps can you take in your local church to begin this process?

Notes

[1]Marcus J. Borg, *The Heart of Christianity: Rediscovering a Life of Faith* (New York: HarperSanFrancisco, 2003), 25.

[2]Dallas Willard, *The Divine Conspiracy: Rediscovering Our Hidden Life in God* (New York: HarperSanFrancisco, 1998), 38.

[3]Ibid., 49.

[4]Harvey Cox, *The Future of Faith* (New York: HarperOne, 2009), 213, 223.

[5]Peter Gomes, *The Scandalous Gospel of Jesus: What's So Good About the Good News?* (New York: HarperOne, 2007), 40-41.

[6]David J. Wolpe, *Why Faith Matters* (New York: HarperOne, 2008), x.

[7]Bob Abernethy and William Bole, *The Life of Meaning: Reflections on Faith, Doubt, and Repairing the World* (New York: Seven Stories, 2007), 337.

[8]Richard Rohr, *Falling Upward: A Spirituality for the Two Halves of Life* (San Francisco: Jossey-Bass, 2011), 13-14.

[9]Dianna Butler Bass, *Christianity After Religion: The End of Church and the Birth of a New Spiritual Awakening* (New York: HarperOne, 2012), 214.

CHAPTER 4

"Redeemed, How I Love to Proclaim It"
(Salvation)

Salvation Is Now

Some Christians have a narrow understanding of salvation that makes it all about the afterlife (going to heaven). They think they know who has it and who doesn't, who's in and who's out, and they consider the work of the church to be largely about converting others to their version of the truth of salvation. At one time, I held to this exclusive version of salvation.

Progressive Christians (and more evangelical Christians are coming to this realization also) insist that there are multiple images and metaphors for salvation in the Scriptures and different, contemporary ways for understanding salvation. Many Christians are surprised to learn that not a single reference to salvation in the Old Testament relates to the afterlife. And only a few references in the New Testament relate specifically to the afterlife.

One of the dominant images in both Testaments is salvation as liberation from bondage. In the Old Testament this is Israel's primal story: Israel's liberation from the domination system of Egypt. Their deliverance set the people of Israel free from a life of victimization and powerlessness. It set them on a journey toward a new land. In the New Testament this is understood primarily as liberation from entrapment, liberation from the anti-human forces of alienation, disintegration, and addiction (what Paul calls the "flesh" and "the law of sin and death").

This image, as it is found in one Gospel story, is particularly illuminating. Just after Jesus predicts for the third time his suffering and death, James and John ask if they can sit by Jesus' side in his kingdom and share Jesus' rule (Mark 10:35-37). This request stirs up the other disciples and continues the bitter dispute they had been having over who would be the greatest (see Mark 9:30-37).

Jesus says, "This is how the prominent people of the world function. They strive for places and positions of power in order to lord it over others. Not so with you. If you want to participate in God's dream for the world, then you must become the servant of all" (my paraphrase of Mark 10:42-44). Then, Jesus offers his own life as an example: "For even the Son of Man did not come to be served, but to serve, and to give his life as a ransom for many" (v. 45).

The word translated "ransom" could also be translated "redemption" or "liberation." Jesus is not specifically speaking of his death, though his death is the culmination of the life he lived. This text is saying that the self-giving, sacrificial life of the Son of Man (Jesus) becomes a means of liberation for his disciples as they follow his way of life.

The afterlife is not in view at all. The liberation in this passage results in freedom from a life of grasping power and position, from the need to lord it over others. The disciples want to turn the old pecking order, where they are on the bottom, into a new pecking order, where they are on the top. Jesus wants to liberate them from the pecking order altogether. He wants to ransom/redeem them from the whole game of competing with and comparing themselves to others, so they will be free to be "servants of all"—without regard or distinction for social status, without bias or prejudice, without favoritism toward any.

Some Christians like to think of salvation only in terms of the afterlife, because then they don't have to struggle with the need to die to the ego-driven self and become a humble servant of all people, which is what Jesus requires. It's much easier and more convenient to make salvation about going to heaven. One hardly has to change at all. Just believe the right doctrines, perform the right rituals, engage in the right practices, and meet the proper criteria in order to secure one's place in the world to come.

Healthy Christianity is about personal, communal, and societal transformation. It's about liberation from egotism, greed, and selfish ambition. It's about reflecting the image of God in all our relationships, embodying the love and compassion of Christ in all we do, and serving all people without discrimination. As Jesus says, it's about being the servant of all (Mark 10:44).

Going Deeper

1. Why is it so difficult for some Christians to imagine salvation in terms other than going to heaven?

2. Marcus Borg, elaborating on the image of the Exodus, wrote: "Liberation brings us into the wilderness. The wilderness is not only a place of freedom beyond the domestication of culture, but also a place of insecurity where we are tempted to erect one golden calf after another."[1] What golden calves are you tempted to pay homage to in your wilderness wanderings?

3. What are some ways our culture holds us in bondage, keeping us from becoming the persons and communities God intends? How can the liberating power of God's love and grace free us from such entanglements?

4. Why is it so difficult to experience freedom from "the whole game of competing with and comparing" ourselves to others?

The Cure for Possession

In the Synoptic Gospels, Jesus' ability to liberate people from the oppression of the demonic functions as a sign of the liberating, healing, whole-making rule of God (Matt 12:28).

From a historical point of view, I'm not sure how to understand all these Gospel stories involving evil spirits. In that day and time, the people had no scientific understanding of infections, diseases, or mental illnesses, attributing their causes to a world of unclean spirits. Jesus, undoubtedly, would have shared that worldview.

But from a spiritual and theological perspective, these stories make perfect sense. We all find ourselves possessed at times by anti-human forces.

When my son was eight years old, I coached his instructional league baseball team in Waldorf, Maryland. Our league was so poor we could not afford umpires, so it fell to the home team to provide them. When we were the hosts, I always tried to pick a parent from both sides to umpire. But on one particular day when we were the visitors, the home team coach and one of its parents were the umpires. (It was an instructional league, but we kept score.)

The ball was hit to our second baseman, which he fielded cleanly, tagged the runner going to second, and then threw the ball to our first baseman for the double play. The runner going to first was fifteen feet away from the bag when the first baseman caught the ball. This was not a judgment call. It was simply what it was—an obvious out.

I turned to the dugout to comment on the play to one of our coaches and when I turned back around, the runner was still standing on first base. I called time out and asked for an explanation. The parent-umpire called the runner safe. He said our first baseman was not on the bag. He made the call while standing behind second base. I was standing on the first base side and saw the play clearly. (This same parent-umpire had called one of his team's players safe on a previous play when our shortstop tagged the runner going to third. He said that our shortstop didn't have the ball in his glove). I appealed to the coach-umpire behind the plate, who, of course, said that he didn't see it and would not overturn the ruling. I found out later that the kid the parent-umpire had called safe at first was his son.

There is more to the story, but no need to hang out my dirty laundry. You know where this is going, don't you? I have no doubt that on that occasion I became possessed by an unclean spirit.

I'm sure you have, too. Have you ever been possessed by anger, by jealousy, by greed or lust, by such a desire to win or accomplish something that you would do whatever you had to do to achieve it? Expressions such as

"I'm not sure what possessed me to do that or to say that" reflect the control these anti-human forces have over us.

Do you know what the cure for possession is? It's possession. Jesus is possessed by the Holy Spirit, so much so that in the Gospel stories his very presence evokes conflict with unholy spirits, the anti-human forces bent on destruction.

As we nurture a relationship with the Spirit, we discover resources that can liberate us from destructive addictions, from negative ingrained habits of attitude and action, from deeply entrenched patterns of behavior that are demeaning and harmful. We acquire from the Spirit the inner resolve to resist the urge to retaliate, and the power to overcome angry outbursts with soft speech and a forgiving demeanor.

The exorcisms in the Gospels are hopeful stories. They are signs that all things demonic, all things that mar and malign God's image in us, all things that degrade, debase, and destroy the "truly human" are on the way out. As disciples of Jesus, we are called to be possessed by the Spirit and fore-shadow God's good, gracious, and just world to come both in our personal lives and in our life together in community.

Going Deeper

1. A fairly consistent theme throughout the New Testament writings is that the Holy Spirit functions as the living presence of Christ. The Spirit takes on the nature and character of Christ. In the Gospel of John, the Spirit is called the Spirit of Truth (see 16:12-15). What truth does the Spirit need to reveal and apply to your life and your faith community in order for you and your church to experience liberation from the anti-human forces that sometimes possess you and your community?

2. In Paul's letter to the Galatians, Paul says that Christians have been set free to love one another, not to live selfishly and to "bite and devour one another" (5:13-15). Next, Paul contrasts life in the "flesh" with life in the Spirit (5:16-26). What characteristics pervade one's life and one's faith community when walking/living by the power of the Spirit?

3. In Ephesians 5, the writer (Paul or someone after Paul within the Pauline tradition) employs the image of intoxication in contrast to being filled with the Spirit (v. 18). A person possessed by alcohol acts foolishly; a person possessed by the Spirit acts wisely, redeeming the time (vv. 15-17). What other characteristics does the writer say are expressed through the possession of the Spirit (vv. 19-21)?

Salvation Is About Life Change

There are several passages in the New Testament that describe Christian salvation in terms of before and after. One such text is Titus 3:3-7.

> For we ourselves were once foolish, disobedient, led astray, slaves to various passions and pleasures, passing our days in malice and envy, despicable, hating one another. But when the goodness and loving kindness of God our Savior appeared, he saved us, not because of any works of righteousness that we had done, but according to his mercy, through the water of rebirth and renewal by the Holy Spirit. The Spirit he poured out on us richly through Jesus Christ our Savior, so that, having been justified by his grace, we might become heirs according to the hope of eternal life.

The contrasts in these texts are somewhat overdrawn, but they are nevertheless real, and they highlight what the early Christians primarily mean when they speak of God's salvation.

Christian salvation means, according to these before-and-after texts, that in Christ and through Christ, we Christians are liberated from negative attitudes and behaviors that are destructive to relationships, communities, and our own souls, as we learn new ways of relating to one another in grace, kindness, and love patterned after Christ. This process of transformation is Christian salvation, not just the result of it.

Christian salvation is not something separate from Christian discipleship. Incorrectly, Christian discipleship has been understood by many American Christians as the consequence of salvation, or something in addition to salvation. This is usually expressed as: We are first saved, and then we are called to live a Christian life. Discipleship is advertised as the next step: If you really want to be serious about it, you will be a disciple. Such a distinction would have been inconceivable to the early Christians.

God calls all Christians to a life of devotion and service in partnership with the Spirit of Christ, and God enables us to realize this calling by delivering us from all those destructive and alienating attitudes and behaviors that diminish and destroy relationships and community. Our living out this calling through the power of the Holy Spirit is what constitutes Christian salvation. When Christian preachers and teachers make salvation primarily about "going to heaven," they do the church a great disservice.

Christian salvation (this process of transformation) is a gift, but like any gift, to be of any use it must be appropriated. According to the text in Titus 3, it is appropriated through the renewing, regenerating, cleansing power of the Holy Spirit that has been generously given to disciples.

The experience of Christian salvation comes about, then, as we are able to respond to the wooing and leading of the Spirit into a life pattern of spiritual awareness and courageous trust. It's largely about letting go of control, and the courage to become what God wants us to be.

Author Sue Monk Kidd recounted the time she volunteered at a shelter for abused children. One day she met Billy, a boy with spiky brown hair and pale eyebrows to match his pale face. The only life in him, said Kidd, was a thirsty look in the half-moons of his eyes. He'd been horribly wounded and was reluctant to go beyond the security he'd found in his room. The day of the Christmas party he shrank against the pillow on his bed and refused to leave the room. Kidd pleaded, "Aren't you coming to the party?" He shook his head.

But then the volunteer beside her spoke up, "Sure you are, Billy. All you need to do is put on your courage skin." His pale eyebrows went up. The thirsty look in his eyes seemed to drink in the possibility. "Okay," he finally said. The volunteer helped him put on an imaginary suit of "courage skin" and off he went to the party, willing to trust and risk beyond his secure places.[2]

Christian salvation is grounded in our surrender to and trust in the living Christ, who beckons us to join his party, who leads us to risk beyond our fears and insecurities, becoming his agents of goodwill in the world. Christ is the lure, calling us forward.

Humanity needs witnesses in order to see the love of God embodied in flesh and blood. With the incarnation of Christ, "the goodness and loving kindness of God our Savior appeared," showing us the way.

Going Deeper

1. The story is told of an elderly southern gentleman who had a rare talent for carving beautiful dogs out of wood. Each day he sat on his porch whittling. One day a visitor asked him about the secret of his art. He said, "I just take a block of wood and whittle off the parts that don't look like a dog." The art of soulmaking involves whittling away the parts of us that diminish our true selves and destroy true community. Can you name those parts of you that need to change? (The first step in exorcising our demons is being able to name them.)

2. A healthy ego, aware of its boundaries, is vital to mental and spiritual wholeness. We all struggle, however, with egocentric patterns that make up our false selves. In numerous ways we seek to defend and protect our egocentric self. These unhealthy patterns of thinking, reacting, and relating to others become habitual and deeply entrenched in our personalities and behavior. What spiritual disciplines might we engage in that would open up our egocentric self to the transforming power of the Spirit?

3. In the letter to the Ephesians the writer speaks of being taught in Christ to put away your "old self" (the false self), the "corrupt and deluded" self, and "to be renewed in the spirit of your minds, and to clothe yourselves with the new self, created according to the likeness of God in true righteousness and holiness." In the next paragraph the writer reveals what that looks like. Reflect on Ephesians 4:21-5:2. What attitudes and actions will we manifest and express when we clothe ourselves with the new self (the true self)?

Conversion Is Possible

The British atheist Malcom Muggeridge joined the Catholic Church at the age of seventy-nine. When he was asked to explain his conversion, he said that all the books and sermons he had read had little, if any, persuasive influence upon him. But when he saw Mother Teresa in Calcutta with the poor, he said, "If this is it, I've got to have it."

On the other hand, Swiss physician Paul Tournier told about going back to his medical school to visit his favorite professor, just after he had written his first book. As they sat in the gathering gloom of a Swiss winter afternoon, Tournier read from his new book. When he finished his reading, he looked up and there were tears in the old man's eyes. "Oh, Paul," he said, "that's a wonderful book. Everyone of us Christians should read that." Tournier was surprised and exclaimed, "I didn't know you were a Christian, professor. When did you become one?" "Just now," he responded, "as you read your book."

I'm sure people of other religious traditions could tell diverse stories of how they were converted into their faith. My argument here is not to push Christianity over other religious faiths, but to point out how God may get our attention and speak to us in various ways and means, and that we all have the capacity to change.

For Muggeridge it was a life lived; for Tournier's professor it was a book read. Somehow God broke through their ego defenses and they were able to hear the voice of the Spirit calling them to embrace a new way of thinking and living.

Of course, authentic conversion/change does not happen just when we initially embrace a new faith—a new way of seeing, belonging, doing, and living. It happens throughout our lives. I was both nurtured and indoctrinated into my faith as a child. There were positive elements within this "nurturing" process, but there were also some very negative components in my dogmatic assimilation into an exclusive version of Christian faith.

Author and speaker Brian McLaren told a story about an African friend who was converted into a type of Christianity that preached a prosperity gospel. Later, he began to have questions, which the leaders in the church stifled. Then he started to doubt the very existence of God.

He decided to read the book, *The God Delusion*, by atheist Richard Dawkins. He reasoned, "If Dawkins convinces me that there is no God, I will abandon my Christian faith." After he read the book, he told McLaren that one evening when he was in the shower the Holy Spirit spoke to him. The voice of God said, "That man, Richard Dawkins, he speaks the truth." (Think of the incongruity of that statement.)

He told McLaren that before the Christian missionaries came they had their own tribal, African understanding of the divine. The missionaries took all that away and gave them a white, European God. What McLaren's friend lost was not his faith in the divine (God), but his faith in the white, European God.

I have discarded most, if not all, of the fundamentalist Christian teachings I was taught in my younger days in order to find a more inclusive, compassionate, and transformational Christian faith. Discarding unhealthy beliefs, so that more life-enhancing ones can emerge, is part of the conversion process.

God is still speaking in a variety of ways, and we can change. We can change our beliefs, along with our negative, destructive attitudes, behaviors, and lifestyles. Our whole lives should be about conversion—our becoming daily more loving, caring, humble, and gracious persons and communities.

Bob Dylan rang out, "The times they are a changin'." His words are as relevant today as when he first sang them in 1964. The times constantly change. We can too!

Going Deeper

1. Simply assenting intellectually to a set of beliefs or doctrines has little, if any, transformative value. But the beliefs we actually hold in our hearts and are willing to entrust and commit our lives to have enormous impact. What core beliefs lie behind your attitudes, decisions, and way of life? Is your lifestyle consistent with what you truly believe in your heart?

2. Do you think faith alone is enough to overcome habitual, addictive attitudes and behavior that are destructive to one's self and relationships? Why or why not?

3. The process of conversion involves the mysterious integration of the divine and human. There are things only God can do, and there are things we must do that God cannot do for us. What is our human responsibility in developing the new/true self and living out the Christ life?

Is God's Future Kingdom a Real Possibility?

How will God's dream for the world (the kingdom of God) be realized in the future? Will it come about by means of a dramatic, divine intervention?

Most Christian interpreters assume that the early church believed Christ would return visibly and personally to judge evil and fulfill the promise of the future kingdom. The teaching found in Mark 13 (ref. Matthew 24, Luke 21) suggests that Jesus expects a dramatic conclusion to the present age and the realization of God's reign on earth in dramatic fashion. Certainly, Paul and the majority of the first Christians hold to an imminent fulfillment of God's kingdom on earth through divine intervention (see 1 Thess. 4:13-5:11, 2 Thess. 2:1-12, 1 Cor. 7:28-31).

The Greek word commonly used to refer to Christ's "coming" is *parousia*, meaning "presence." Of course, if someone is absent and later becomes present, then that person has "come back" or "returned." But in one sense, Jesus never left. In the New Testament, the Spirit functions as the equivalent of the living presence of Christ in the church and in the world. Understood in this light, Jesus' "coming" is not an invasion from the outside, but an unveiling, manifesting, and appearing from within.

New Testament scholar N. T. Wright has argued that the language of the Son of Man coming in the clouds of heaven denotes Christ's exaltation, not his return. As far as I can tell, no serious New Testament scholar adopts this exegetical approach to the apocalyptic language of Christ's "coming," though I, with Wright, personally find it a stretch to imagine Jesus returning as "a kind of space invader to sort out a rebel planet."

Even though the early Christians (oriented as they were around a cosmology of a flat earth under a heavenly dome) understood Jesus' "coming" quite literally, there is no reason why Christians today must maintain the belief that Jesus will descend from another world to earth to usher in the kingdom supernaturally. Perhaps God's reign will be implemented through the power of the Spirit working in conjunction and collaboration with Christ's agents and emissaries of justice and peace in the world.

Some progressive Christians contend that the more likely scenario for the realization of God's new world is found in the dynamic dance of the Spirit with humanity, empowering and energizing disciples of Christ (the church) and others, regardless of religious tradition or belief, to confront the powers that be and to engage the world through suffering love, compassionate justice, and nonviolent peacemaking.

It is, however, a legitimate question to ask whether the realization of God's new world as envisaged by Jesus and his early followers is actually possible. There is no doubt that humanity has evolved in its cumulative spiritual consciousness, inspiring visions of a more compassionate, equal, and just world. Still, there are powerfully destructive and evil forces set against the fulfillment of God's new world. At this stage in our spiritual evolution, it is just as easy to imagine a cataclysmic nuclear or chemical holocaust as it is to imagine a world of righteousness and peace.

A just world would be a world where all God's children have enough— not only enough to survive, but also to thrive, to live a flourishing life. There would be equitable distribution of resources, and love of neighbor would prevail. When we consider the rampant greed and egotism, as well as the stark global, national, political, economic, social, and religious polarization among peoples of this earth, it's hard to imagine the kingdom of God being realized through gradual spiritual growth and transformation.

Is the vision of God's new world on earth a real possibility? Or is it just a "wish upon a star" with little real hope of actuality?

There are moments when I experience this hope as a genuine possibility; other times, though, it seems more like a vain wish. I honestly don't know how to imagine the realization of God's kingdom on earth. In terms of our spiritual evolution as a species we are at a child's level. We certainly are not past adolescence.

Disciples of Jesus, however, need not worry about how life on this planet will conclude. It is enough to know that God is with us and for us, and that God is constantly wooing, drawing, and inviting us into participation with God's good will for the planet today and toward a hopeful tomorrow. As disciples of Jesus, we are committed to his vision of a transformed world and are responsible for interacting with the Spirit as we engage in works of healing, justice, peacemaking, and compassion—whatever the final outcome for our planet will be.

I am convinced, however, that nothing we do for the healing and transformation of our world—no kindness, no act of justice on behalf of the oppressed, no act of forgiveness, no loving word or deed—will be lost. I am confident that God's vindication/resurrection of Jesus, who embodied God's new world, is God's pledge that abundant life will overcome the malignant powers of death.

Going Deeper

1. It would seem that Jesus and his first followers believed in an imminent fulfillment of God's kingdom (Mark 9:1, 13:30; 1 Cor. 7:28-31; 1 Thess. 4:17). Obviously, they were wrong. Luke seems to tackle the issue of God's delay in the realization of the kingdom in passages such as Luke 19:11-27 and Acts 1:6-8. Could the early Christians have been wrong about the fulfillment of the kingdom altogether? If you were to become convinced that the kingdom of God, as Jesus and the early Christians envisioned it, would never be realized on earth, would that make a difference in your commitment to see it realized? Would you stop praying and working for its realization?

2. However we imagine the ultimate redemption of the world, it's important to note that the early Christians believed it extended to all creation. Read and reflect on Romans 8:18-25. How does Paul, in this passage, imagine future redemption? What bearing should this have on how we treat the planet and other living creatures now?

3. The prophetic outlook that compelled the *Left Behind* books anticipates a global holocaust as a prerequisite for Christ's return. Some adherents of this view can hardly hide their excitement when forebodings of catastrophic happenings are in the air. Is this healthy? What are the moral and spiritual problems with apocalyptic schemes?

God's Loving Judgment

Unconditional love means unconditional acceptance, but it does not mean unconditional approval. God loves us regardless, but God certainly doesn't approve of all we do. God doesn't approve when we take advantage of others and perform deeds of injustice. God doesn't approve when we act and react in selfish ways that hurt others. God doesn't approve of our many expressions of pride and egotism. Such attitudes and actions grieve God and are in direct opposition to God's will.

But God continues to love us, even though God may be saddened or angered by what we do. God never writes us off. God is patient and waits like a loving parent for the return of a lost child (Luke 15:11-24). The Hebrew prophets, who often speak of God's anger, never speak of an angry God, as if anger is an essential part of God's disposition. God gets angry, but God's anger soon passes. God's love endures forever (Jer. 31:3, 33:11; Hos. 2:19; Isa. 26:20; Mic. 7:18-20). As the psalmist declares, "God's anger is but for a moment; his favor is for a lifetime" (Ps. 30:5).

Covenant is a dominant theme in both the Hebrew Bible and the Christian Testament. Covenants express, at different stages in the biblical story, God's relationship to God's people. God is bound by covenant to the creation and to all God's children.

It is my contention that God's judgment is not incompatible with God's love. We have no idea what God's judgment consists of really. It may be, mostly, God allowing us to reap the consequences of our actions. Or, perhaps, sometimes it takes the form of more direct, specific, divine involvement. We have all heard the phrase "tough love." The expression implies that love can be painful, difficult, and hard to bear at times. Loving parents may have to enforce some rather strict measures of discipline. The wife of an alcoholic husband may have to obtain a restraining order or even press legal charges in order to protect their children or get her husband the help he needs.

God's judgment is always a form of love. It is nothing like the sentence or penalty of condemnation rendered from a non-feeling jury or judge. God is always partial toward our ultimate well-being. Judgment is never retributive or strictly punitive. It is always corrective, redemptive, and restorative. The ultimate intent of God's judgment is to heal, redeem, reconcile, and transform. That may or may not be possible for all people, but it is God's intent.

If judgment is anything else, it would nullify the gospel of grace. One afternoon when Jordan, my son, was a toddler, he was with me as I picked up a few household items at K-Mart. I told him he could pick out something for himself within our tight budget. (In those days it was very tight.) He wanted some kind of action figure that was more expensive than what we could afford. As I tried to explain that he would need to scale back, he threw a little fit in the store.

I looked him squarely in the eyes and informed him that if he didn't settle down, he wouldn't be getting anything. He didn't settle down. So, I took it all off the table. Then he wanted to compromise. He picked something else out when he knew I was serious. I told him it was too late. As we made our way through the store, he was so sad and mad he couldn't see straight.

Well, I began to have a change of heart. I thought this could be a teachable moment. So I went back, with Jordan unaware, and slipped into the cart the second item he had chosen. When we returned to the car and after I put him in his car seat, I pulled out the toy and surprised him with it. I said, "Son, this is called grace. You don't deserve it, but in my love for you, I decided to get it for you anyway." I don't think he was old enough to understand the Christian concept of grace, but he sure was delighted to get the toy. And his delight was my delight. The hug he gave me to seal the whole experience made my heart melt. It demonstrates the healing, transformative power of grace.

God's love and grace constitute God's settled disposition toward God's children; God's judgment is merely an instrument of God's grace. The Hebrew scholar and spiritual writer Abraham Heschel observed, "The anger of the Lord is instrumental, hypothetical, conditional, and subject to His will. Let the people modify their line of conduct, and anger will disappear . . . There is no divine anger for anger's sake . . . its purpose and consummation is its own disappearance."[3]

Since God's judgment is an expression of God's love, then there is nothing to fear. Whatever God's judgment may involve, no matter how painful it may be at the time, it is intended for our ultimate good.

Going Deeper

1. In most apocalyptic visions of the future a kind of general judgment is envisioned. Do you believe in a future general judgment? Why or why not?

2. What are the basic differences between retributive/punitive theological frameworks for understanding judgment and those that are restorative/redemptive in nature?

3. Abraham Heschel wrote: "The call to anger is a call to cancel anger. It is not an expression of irrational, sudden, and instinctive excitement, but a free and deliberate reaction of God's justice to what is wrong and evil."[4] In your own words, explain what you think Heschel meant by "the call to anger is a call to cancel anger." Why does God get angry? What does God want to accomplish through anger?

Wendell Berry and the Afterlife

Wendell Berry's novel, *A World Lost*, told a story about a family coping with the death of one of their own. In the final chapter, Berry reflected on the manner of man he was. That meditation gave way to a reflection on death as a pathway into the light of a more advanced spiritual realm. Berry wrote:

> I imagine the dead waking, dazed, into a shadowless light in which they know themselves altogether for the first time. It is a light that is merciless until they can accept its mercy; by it they are at once condemned and redeemed. It is Hell until it is Heaven. Seeing themselves in that light, if they are willing, they see how far they have failed the only justice of loving one another; it punishes them by their own judgment. And yet, in suffering that light's awful clarity, in seeing themselves within it, they see its forgiveness and its beauty, and are consoled. In it they are loved completely, even as they have been, and so are changed into what they could not have been but what, if they could have imagined it, they would have wished to be.[5]

How I wish more Christians would apply Berry's good reasoning, common sense, imagination, insight into human experience, and his healthy image of the divine to their interpretations of the judgment texts in Scripture.

Berry said that "light can come into the world only as love" and that "not enough light has ever reached us here among the shadows," and yet "it has never been entirely absent."[6]

When divine love finally reaches us and has its final say, "All will be well."

If we could grasp and trust Berry's vision, then our biblical images of judgment would not be so terrifying. We might be able to replace our tormenting images with purifying images, invested with new meaning. Our fear might then give way to hope.

The "furnace of fire" would be a furnace that burns up all the dross, leaving the precious metal. The fire would consume our sin and selfishness, bringing us through the flames purged and pure.

The journey through "outer darkness" would serve to dispel the inner darkness and illumine our minds and hearts to the mystery, wonder, and power of God's goodness and grace.

The "weeping and gnashing of teeth" would be a necessary prelude to the joy and celebration that result from the experience of grace and real gratitude.

We need the darkness as preparation for the light. At first, the light may feel like a condemning light. But it is a condemnation that leads to salvation, and passing through "hell" we reach "heaven."

The journey of personal redemption is a journey from the selfish ways of childhood to the adulthood of self-giving love. It is a journey from the partial to the complete, from immaturity to maturity, from brokenness to wholeness, from the false self to the true self, from egoism to compassion, from exclusive focus on our own suffering to an inclusive solidarity with the suffering creation, especially our disadvantaged sisters and brothers within the human family.

Each journey is unique. Each has its own twists and turns, defeats and victories, setbacks and advances. None of the "hells" we each pass through are exactly alike. But I am convinced that the God who has come to us in Jesus, who knows the number of hairs on our heads, who calls us "dearly beloved," will bring each one of us to final redemption.

Going Deeper

1. Theologian Jürgen Moltmann wrote: "Only when the apocalyptic expectation of judgment is completely Christianized does it lose its terror and become a liberating hope, in which we go to meet the future with heads held high . . . Then the fear of judgment will no longer hinder and paralyze the expectation of the parousia."[7] In my article above, apocalyptic images of judgment are "Christianized" into more hopeful and liberating images. Do you agree or disagree with this reimaging and reinterpreting of the biblical/apocalyptic images? Why?

2. Read and reflect on Luke 6:27-36. Jesus calls his followers to love their enemies because God loves God's enemies. Does this image of God, as well as Jesus' experience of God as *Abba*, a loving, compassionate parent, impact how you understand God's judgment?

3. Scholars have noted that when the judgment texts in the Synoptic Gospels are compared, most all of the severe, harsh images of judgment are found in Matthew's Gospel in contradiction to Matthew's own dominant portrait of Jesus. Apparently the author or editor/redactor of Matthew's Gospel had an ax to grind. Why is it such a struggle for so many Christians to let go of their harsh, vengeful, terrifying images of judgment?

Notes

[1] Marcus Borg, *The Heart of Christianity: Rediscovering a Life of Faith* (New York: HarperSanFrancisco, 2003), 176.

[2] Sue Monk Kid, *When the Heart Waits: Spiritual Direction for Life's Sacred Questions* (New York: HarperSanFrancisco, 1990), 109.

[3] Abraham Joshua Heschel, *The Prophets, II* (Peabody, MA: Hendrickson Publishers, 1962), 66.

[4] Ibid.

[5] Wendell Berry, *A World Lost* (Berkeley, CA: Counterpoint, 2008), 104.

[6] Ibid.

[7] Jürgen Moltmann, *The Way of Jesus Christ: Christology in Messianic Dimensions*, trans. Margaret Kohl (Minneapolis: Fortress Press, 1993), 315.

CHAPTER 5

Walking the Talk
(Discipleship)

Followers of the Way

In the book of Acts, Luke says that Paul, who is "still breathing threats and murder against the disciples of the Lord," goes into Damascus looking for those "who belonged to the Way" (9:1-2). This is how the first Christians are known: They are "disciples" of Jesus committed to his "way" of life, the way of God's kingdom that Jesus himself embodies (Luke 17:20-21).

The early Christians understand that to be a disciple of Jesus means involvement in a process of learning how to walk in the way of Jesus—a way of simplicity, humility, inclusivity, forgiveness, nonviolence, compassion, and commitment to a greater good, the kingdom of God.

Today there are numerous versions of Christian faith that hardly resemble the above description. They make doctrinal and creedal conformity central (some even denounce as false teachers anyone who would preach or teach a different version than their own) and place most of the emphasis on the afterlife.

I remember in my youth being part of a revival effort, wearing a button that had a picture of a hand and finger pointing upward with the caption, "Jesus is the way." But if you had asked me then what that meant, I would have said either of two things. I would have told you that Jesus is the way to heaven for anyone who would accept him as their personal Savior, or I would have said that Jesus is the way to a happy and meaningful life (understood in terms of a self-fulfilling life). I had no idea then what I know now about the actual way of Jesus in the world—his commitment to the poor and marginalized, his embrace of outsiders, his insistence on nonviolence, his call to love our enemies, his radical teaching on unconditional forgiveness, and his constant readiness to challenge the injustice of the political and religious powers.

We have distorted the gospel of Jesus. We have given sincere believers doctrines, dogmas, and creeds and incorporated them into church systems that have been more about control, management, and growing the institution than about living the life of Jesus and pursuing the way of Jesus in the world. But then, we didn't know any better. No one ever told us. We were only passing on the Christian faith as it had been passed on to us.

I am hopeful, though, because there seems to be a growing emergence (this emergence has been happening for some time in other places such as the Global South) in Western Christianity of the faith of Jesus, faith expressed through love (Gal. 5:6). There seems to be a slowly expanding minority of Christians who are taking seriously Jesus' vision of a transformed world, who are attempting to put into practice the attitudes and actions, the life and vision of Jesus. Time will tell what impact this effort will have.

In the days ahead, if Christians are to have any credibility and authenticity with spiritual seekers who are peace-loving, clear-thinking, and who care about creation, equality, and issues of justice for the most vulnerable among us, then it will be to the extent that we actually pursue and practice "the way" of Jesus.

I hope, as a species created to bear the image of God, that in the future we will more visibly and clearly reflect that image. I feel confident that we are evolving past the days of the Crusades, Inquisitions, witch hunts, and heresy trials. Christians can be a major force for good on this planet if we can move past exclusive, belief-centered, condemnatory Christianity and embrace a more grace-filled, inclusive vision of the cosmic Christ who is ever present in the world and who resides with and in each person (John 1:9).

Going Deeper

1. Jesus called people to repentance as part of his announcement of the good news of God's kingdom (Mark 1:14-15). Repentance involves a process of turning or returning to God. It involves a change of mind and direction that inspires a new way of seeing, relating, and living. For Christians, this involves allegiance to the way of Jesus. Repentance is both a beginning and a journey. What areas of your life call for repentance (change of mind, attitude, direction, behavior, and lifestyle) in order to embody the way of Jesus?

2. Jesus was a boundary breaker. He overstepped and disregarded purity laws by eating with sinners and tax collectors, healing on the Sabbath, touching lepers, and healing the diseased and demonized. He broke down barriers of race, extending grace to Samaritans and Gentiles. He broke down barriers of gender by calling women disciples and treating women as equals with the utmost dignity and respect. In numerous ways he confronted the status quo, challenging unhealthy and demeaning religious practices. In what ways will we function as boundary breakers today if we embody and follow the way of Jesus?

3. Possibly the most difficult challenge of all in following the way of Jesus is pursuing his way of nonviolence. Jesus endured the cross, absorbing and bearing the hate, prejudice, and violence without returning it upon his tormentors. Are you committed to the way of nonviolence? If not, how do you harmonize your discipleship to Jesus with Jesus' call to love our enemies and to follow him on his nonviolent path to the cross (Matt 5:43-48; Mark 8:31-35)?

Joel Osteen and the Scandalous Gospel of Jesus

Joel Osteen has been deemed by many as America's pastor. He is pastor of the largest church in America, and his books have sold in the millions. I scanned Joel Osteen's book, *Your Best Life Now*, in search of any serious reflection or teaching on the life, teaching, and death of Jesus and his call to discipleship presented in the Gospels. It's not there.

That's not to say that Osteen doesn't have some good things to say. For example, he talks about developing a healthy self-image, cultivating a positive outlook, and claiming one's worth and value as a child of God—all very good things. But his emphasis on personal success seems to fly in the face of the gospel of Jesus. He writes:

> If you will keep the right attitude, God will take all your disappointments, broken dreams, the hurts and pains, and He'll add up all the trouble and sorrow that's been inflicted upon you, and He will pay you back with twice as much peace, joy, happiness, and success . . . If you just believe, if you'll put your trust and confidence in God, He will give you double for your trouble.[1]

Really, brother Joel, double for my trouble? Is that what Jesus says?

In the Gospels, Jesus tells his disciples that because he is persecuted they can expect to be persecuted too, since the servant is not greater than the master (John 15:20). Jesus turns the values of the world on their head when he says, "Blessed are those who are persecuted for righteousness' sake, for theirs is the kingdom of heaven" (Matt. 5:11). Jesus rebukes his disciples for desiring upward mobility and worldly versions of success: "You know that among the Gentiles those whom they recognize as their rulers lord it over them. But it is not so among you; but whoever wishes to become great among you must be your servant . . . For the Son of Man came not to be served, but to serve" (Mark 10:42-44). Jesus tells his disciples, "In the world you face persecution. But take courage: I have conquered the world!" (John 16:33). Jesus overcomes the world, not through worldly success, but through worldly defeat, through the suffering love endured on the cross, through bearing the hate and violence of the world without returning that hate and violence.

Jesus says in Luke's Gospel, "Woe to you who are rich, for you have already received your comfort. Woe to you who are well fed now, for you will go hungry. Woe to you who laugh now, for you will mourn and weep. Woe to you when everyone speaks well of you, for that is how their ancestors treated the false prophets" (6:24-26). How do these words of woe on the wealthy and comfortable fit a gospel of success?

Please don't misunderstand me: I am not knocking anyone's desire to be successful in work, career, education, or any other endeavor. As far as I am concerned, the desire to be successful within the boundaries of an honest, humble, caring, compassionate, and generous life is a noble aspiration. But let's be clear: It is not the gospel of Jesus.

Osteen says, "Think big. Think increase. Think abundance. Think more than enough." Following his statement on personal success, he tells this story:

Years ago, a famous golfer was invited by the king of Saudi Arabia to play in a golf tournament. He accepted the invitation, and the king flew his private jet in to pick him up. After the event, as the golfer was getting on the plane to return to the United States, the king told him that he would like to give him a gift for making this time so special. The golfer told the king that a gift was not necessary, but the king insisted. So the golfer said, "Well, I collect golf clubs. Why don't you get me a golf club?"

On his flight back, the golfer wondered what sort of golf club the king might get him. A few weeks later a certified letter came in the mail from the king of Saudi Arabia. The golfer at first wondered what this had to do with a golf club. When he opened the envelope, to his great surprise, he discovered a deed to a 500-acre golf course in America. Pretty nice golf club, don't you think? Osteen writes, "We serve the Most High God, and His dream for your life is so much bigger and better than you can even imagine. It's time to enlarge your vision!"[2]

Certainly Jesus challenges us to enlarge our vision, but is that Jesus' vision? A 500-acre golf course? Personal success and fulfillment? Is that the greater story and larger vision Jesus intended through his proclamation of the "the kingdom of God"?

In the Synoptic Gospels, Jesus tells his disciples on three different occasions that he, the Son of Man, is going to be rejected, suffer many things, and be killed. On the first occasion when Jesus breaks the news, he then tells them, "If any want to become my followers, let them deny themselves and take up their cross and follow me. For those who want to save their life will lose it, and those who lose their life for my sake, and for the sake of the gospel will save it" (Mark 8:34-35). This call to discipleship comes at a critical juncture in the story and sets the pattern for a life of discipleship to Jesus.

I don't believe God calls us to be poor. Some individuals and communities, like the Franciscans, are called to such a lifestyle. Generally speaking, though, I believe God wants all of God's children, all across the world, to have enough—not only to survive, but also to thrive—to live a flourishing life. That will never happen by merely following Osteen's teaching of pursuing your personal best.

Jesus' call to discipleship is a call to pursue the way of the cross. It's not about gain and glory; it's not about acquisition and acclamation; it's not about self-fulfillment and success. It's about self-denial and taking up one's cross. That doesn't mean there is no joy. There's plenty of joy, real joy, but not the kind of joy that money and power can buy, not the kind of joy that comes through being successful and happy by American standards. That's the paradox of the gospel; there is joy, peace, and inner contentment in the way of the cross, but it is not found on the path to personal success. It is found on the path of self-surrender, self-sacrifice, and service to others.

Going Deeper

1. There is no way to avoid the comparing and competing to win at the expense of others that is the result of a gospel of personal success. In what ways are the common human activities of competing and comparing that are so common in our society detrimental to a healthy spiritual life based on the way of Jesus?

2. In a picture book for adults by Trina Paulus, Yellow (a yellow caterpillar) came upon a gray-haired caterpillar who told her about becoming a butterfly. When she asked how to become one, he responded, "You must want to fly so much that you are willing to give up being a caterpillar." Yellow asked, "You mean to die?" Gray said, "Yes and no. What *looks like you* will die but *what's really you* will still live."[3] In order to really live in the spiritual world of God's kingdom and pursue the way of Jesus, we must relinquish some things. What do you need to die to in order to follow the way of Jesus?

3. In 2010 a small group from our church went to Zambia. We help support the work of missionaries Lonnie and Fran Turner through their "Partners in Development" project. A key component of their work is providing fresh water to villages by digging wells. A member from our group noted that Zambia did not have a water problem. The water table is high, and most wells do not require a lot of digging. Their problem is not a resource problem, but a distribution problem. And that, of course, is a problem all over the world. What must happen individually, communally, nationally,

and globally in order to solve the distribution problem? In what ways are we complicit in the problem? What can we do as individuals and as churches to contribute to the solution and be advocates of policies that more fairly distribute the world's resources so that all God's children have enough, not only to survive, but also to thrive?

God May Make Christians of Us Yet

In his autobiography, *Brother to a Dragonfly*, Will Campbell recounted the experience that caused him to confront the radical implications of the gospel of reconciliation. His friend, civil rights worker Jonathan Daniels, had just been gunned down in cold blood by volunteer Deputy Sheriff Thomas Coleman in Lowndes County, Alabama. Will was livid with grief and rage over Jonathan's murder.

In the aftermath, Will's agnostic friend, P. D. East, reminded Will of a conversation they had years earlier. P. D. had challenged Will to give him a definition of the Christian faith in ten words or less. Will defined it this way: "We are all bastards, but God loves us anyway." P. D. now challenged Will's succinct definition of the gospel.

P. D. tore into Will, "Was Jonathan a bastard?" Will commented on how Jonathan was one of the sweetest, most gentle guys he had ever known. P. D. pressed, "But was he a bastard?"—his tone almost a scream. Will knew P. D. had him cornered. Will finally conceded, "Yes." P. D. came firing back, "All right. Is Thomas Coleman a bastard?" That was easy. "Yes, Thomas Coleman is a bastard."

P. D. said, "Okay, let me get this straight . . . Jonathan Daniels was a bastard. Thomas Coleman is a bastard. . . . Which of these two bastards do you think God loves the most? Does God love that little dead bastard Jonathan the most? Or does he love the living bastard Thomas the most?"

The truth of the gospel hit Will with such force that he described the encounter as something of a conversion experience. Will was overcome with emotion. He found himself weeping and laughing simultaneously. He told P. D., "Damn, Brother, if you haven't gone and made a Christian out of me."[4]

The gospel of reconciliation is a radical gospel; it is offensive to conservatives, moderates, and liberals alike. To think that God loves a Thomas Coleman as much as a Jonathan Daniels is hard to take, isn't it?

I have no doubt this is why so many liberals have equated the gospel with a social cause and so many conservatives have reduced the gospel to going to heaven when we die or privatized it into a gospel of personal fulfillment or holiness. Institutional Christianity, on both the right and left, has a tough time with this radical gospel of unconditional love and grace.

Paul says in his correspondence with the church in Corinth that God was in Christ reconciling the world to God's self, not counting their transgressions against them (2 Cor. 5:19). All are loved and forgiven. Thomas Coleman and Jonathan Daniels, Hitler and Mother Teresa—all are God's children.

How do we live this scandalous gospel? It's not easy. I know I cannot do it on my own. It's easy to identify with the victim, but to love the perpetrator of abuse or violence takes more love than I am capable of. I need grace. I need to "know" at the deep, core level of my being, beyond my intellect, the love of God that passes all understanding.

Only through fresh encounters with the divine love that pervades and sustains all reality—that we Christians believe became incarnate in Jesus of Nazareth—can we find the faith, strength, courage, and hope to love the Thomas Colemans' of the world.

Going Deeper

1. Do you agree that "only through fresh encounters with the divine love that became incarnate in Jesus of Nazareth" can we begin to actually love the Thomas Colemans' of the world? Why or why not?

2. United States Congressman John Lewis was a major leader in the Civil Rights Movement. In his book, *Across That Bridge,* he wrote: "Even though we had been rejected by society, we believed that all people had the capacity to be good. We believed not only we, but the perpetrators of violence, were victims as well, who began their lives in innocence but were taught to hate, abuse, and draw distinctions between themselves and others. We held no malice toward them and believed in the power of the truth to penetrate that negative conditioning and remind people of their innocence once again."[5] Can such faith as described above empower us to love our enemies and the perpetrators of violence? What will it take spiritually for us to possess such faith and love?

3. Why do so many of us deny or ignore this radical gospel of reconciliation? How do many Christians rationalize and justify acts of violence?

God Suffers with Our Suffering World

When Rob Bell, author of *Love Wins*, was interviewed by Martin Bashir of MSNBC, Bashir asked Bell to respond to the earthquake disaster in Japan. Bashir phrased the question this way, "Which do you believe: That God is all-powerful, but doesn't care about the people in Japan and their suffering, or that God cares about their suffering, but is not all-powerful?" He framed the question as if these were the only two options.

Bell responded by saying that he begins with the belief that when we shed a tear, God sheds a tear; that God is a divine being who is profoundly empathetic, compassionate, and stands in solidarity with us. That response, however, did not fit Bashir's binary, dualistic way of thinking, so he kept pressing Bell. Finally, Bell responded, "It's a paradox at the heart of the divine, and it's best left at that."

Bashir framed his questions in a way that required either/or, yes/no, true/false responses. Yet the questions dealt with truth that defied such simplistic answers. (Jesus, by the way, never offers simplistic answers. He speaks in parables and stories; in short, witty aphorisms; in shocking, hyperbolic sayings filled with paradox, irony, and mystery.) Healthy Christianity—or any religion for that matter—does not need or invite simple, trite, all-encompassing answers to the universal questions of human suffering and meaning.

Christianity does not have easy answers, but it does have the cross, where God in Christ enters into the tragedy of the human condition and bears it, endures it, owns it, and absorbs it.

In his novel *Jayber Crow*, Wendell Berry observed that Christ did not descend from the cross except into the grave, and that God is present "only in the ordinary miracle of the existence of God's creatures." Berry has a way of cutting against the grain of our privatized, compartmentalized way of seeing life, reflecting a more universal and inclusive worldview. He wrote, "We are all involved in all and any good, and in all and any evil. For any sin, we all suffer. That is why our suffering is endless. It is why God grieves and Christ's wounds still are bleeding."[6]

It is in Christ's once-upon-a-cross humiliation and in his ever-present bleeding wounds that we find a brother. In his cry of abandonment upon the cross, "My God, my God, why have you forsaken me?" we have a comrade and friend. Christ descends into our "hell" and suffers it, in order to empty it of its malevolent power, so that we who follow Christ through our own "hells" can find healing and redemption through his suffering and death.

Our disappointments and discouragements, our losses and defeats, our feelings of rejection and forsakenness do not separate us from God, but draw us into fellowship with God and one another through the sufferings of Christ. As theologian Jürgen Moltmann said, "Good Friday is the most comprehensive and most profound expression of Christ's fellowship with every human being."[7]

Paul says that "in Christ God was reconciling the world to God's self, not counting their trespasses against them" (2 Cor. 5:19). Christ bears the hate, evil, and animosity of the world without returning it, and therefore stands in union and solidarity with every suffering soul.

In the passion narrative of the Gospels, Jesus is totally passive, bearing it all, but God is active in, with, and for Jesus, suffering with our suffering world. God is still active in and through the Spirit of the living Christ, sharing our sorrow, feeling our pain, and participating in every loss and humiliation.

Going Deeper

1. Suffering as a means of spiritual growth is well attested in the biblical tradition (see Jas. 1:2-4, Rom. 5:1-5, 1 Pet. 1:6-9). Sometimes recovering addicts will talk about their addiction as "a necessary suffering" that helped to bring them spiritual and emotional health. It was something they could not control, manage, fix, or even explain, and it forced them into a teachable place and opened them up to be formed by a greater Power. Why does it usually take some form of suffering to cause us to let go of our egocentric preoccupations and advance us in our spiritual development? Can you name a crisis in your life that compelled you to grow in character and to expand your spiritual awareness?

2. In Philippians 2:10-11, Paul links the experience of Christ's risen life with participation in his sufferings, and in Romans 8:17 he says that we share in Christ's sufferings "in order that we may share in his glory." In these passages Paul apparently is talking about an intentional sharing in the sufferings of Christ. Most likely, this involves an intentional solidarity and deliberate identification with those who are suffering, especially those suffering from injustice. Our willingness to enter into the hurt, loss, and pain of others may be the single most important thing that opens us up to the compassion and love of Christ. Obviously, we are limited in how much of this we can bear, both as individuals and as faith communities, but we must do some of this. What steps can you and your church take to deliberately and purposefully share in the suffering and pain of others?

3. Life is unfair and some people suffer far more than others due to no fault of their own. The gospel of Jesus does not give us answers or explanations, but it does give us the cross. How is the cross of Jesus helpful?

Discovering Our True Vocation

In the Gospels, Jesus' sense of vocation—his conviction about what he is called to do—emerges from a clear sense of who he is.

Before Jesus begins his public ministry he most likely is a follower of John the Baptist. He is baptized by John in the desert. In the context of his baptismal experience Jesus is given a vision, a revelation of his true self. The Gospels employ symbolic language to describe Jesus' spiritual encounter: The heavens opened, the Spirit descended in the appearance of a dove, and the divine voice pronounced, "You are my Son, the Beloved; with you I am well pleased" (Mark 1:11).

Immediately after his mystical encounter with God, Jesus faces Satan in the desert. There Jesus encounters both wild beasts and angels (Mark 1:13), that is, the ego enticements that could derail his mission and the divine provision that would enable him to stay the course. Jesus experiences the temptations to be relevant, spectacular, and powerful in the execution of his mission (Matt. 4:1-11); temptations that would continue to confront him from time to time as he remains faithful to God's will. In the power of the Spirit (Luke 4:14) he heals the diseased and demonized, proclaims the good news of the kingdom of God, and welcomes all manner of sinners and outcasts into his fellowship.

Jesus becomes the messianic agent of God's reign and dream for the world after he hears the still, small voice of the Spirit affirming him as God's Son. Jesus models a pattern that can guide us into true vocation.

Dennis Lynn is an author and spiritual retreat leader. Having been brought up in a very strict religious environment, his primary goal in life as an adolescent was to avoid hell. He tried to avoid the long list of sins that he had been taught would lead to his eternal banishment. He grew up hating himself and not liking anyone else much either.

A major change took place in his life when he joined the Jesuits. His novice master had instructed him to make a general confession of his sins. He wrote twelve pages of all the things he didn't like about himself. At his confession, Dennis started with page one and talked non-stop for thirty minutes.

At the end of his confession, his novice master said nothing. Instead, he came over and gave Dennis a big hug. It was then that the heavens opened, the Spirit descended, and he heard the voice of God affirming that he was God's son, that God loved him no matter what.[8]

Dennis' experience of being loved unconditionally as God's child led to his conviction about his true vocation. From then on Dennis felt he could be a brother to all people, that he could love a lot because he had been forgiven a lot—at least twelve pages worth.

I have often contended that doubts and questions are essential for our spiritual growth. My doubts and questions certainly spurred me to dig deeper, which led to a stronger faith and a more compassionate life.

However, there is one truth that I hope I never doubt: *the truth that God loves us as we are.* We belong to God and are God's daughters and sons, no matter how many faults and failures mark our path, no matter how destructive our addictions or confusing our problems.

Regardless of how much we achieve, how many accolades, honors, or awards we earn, God will not love us any more than God loves us right now. And no matter how badly we mess up or how many sins characterize our lives, God will not love us any less than God loves us right now.

As we claim our identity as God's beloved children, our vocation (calling) begins to take shape. Knowing who we are, we are awakened to a clearer sense of what we are to be about.

Going Deeper

1. Our culture prepares and pressures us to participate in an economic system based on competition, comparison, and profit at the expense of others. As a result, many link their identity to how much money they make and to the number of accolades they receive. The culture tells them who they are. Who tells you who you are? Is your identity tied to the titles you have acquired, the status you have achieved, the money you have earned, or the control and power you have wielded over others? How might you go about finding your true value, worth, and identity in God alone?

2. Conformity to the mold of the economic, political, social, and religious systems of the world results in a hurried, frenzied, chaotic life. Relinquishment to a bigger cause (the kingdom of God), participation in a larger story of service and ministry to others, and surrender to a greater purpose result in inner peace, gratitude, increased vitality, and purposeful living (see Rom 12:1-2, Phil 4:4-9). What attitudes do you need to change and what steps do you need to take in order to move from a place of busy, burdened conformity to the world to a place of restful, grateful being and meaningful, purposeful doing as a beloved child of God?

3. What is it you have to do that you can't not do? (Be as honest and open and truthful as you are able.) Your sincere response to that question will tell you a lot about where you are on your spiritual journey.

Finding Our Rhythm

The life of Jesus as presented in the Gospels demonstrates a rhythm of prayer/ spiritual retreat and worldly engagement that is critical to a healthy, holistic, spiritual life. The pattern of discipleship that Jesus models is one of solitude and service. Throughout his ministry Jesus moves back and forth between spiritual retreat and active ministry.

There are a number of personal, inner disciplines that nurture the spiritual life: study, spiritual reading, theological reflection, confession, self-examination, silence, solitude, meditation, and of course, the many forms and expressions of prayer.

It is largely through these personal, spiritual disciplines that disciples of Jesus find strength to endure the pain of life, the wisdom to guide and sustain them along the way, the courage to cope with difficult challenges, and the hope to inspire them not to give up. Through these disciplines of the Spirit, disciples of Jesus open their lives to the divine Spirit, to the grace and transforming love of God, and find the power, motivation, passion, and courage to engage the world as servants and ministers of the living Christ.

I like what was told the stranger who happened to attend a Quaker meeting by mistake. He waited patiently in the Quaker silence for things to get started. Five minutes turned into ten; then, when he could bear it no longer, he asked the person seated next to him, "When does the service begin?" The Quaker responded, "When the worship ends." Whatever form our "worship" takes, it should connect us with the divine love in a way that empowers us to live a compassionate life of kindness and service to others.

Preacher and former seminary professor Dr. Fred Craddock told about the time, when as a freshman at Johnson Bible College in Tennessee, he heard Rear Admiral Thornton Miller speak in chapel. Admiral Miller was the highest ranking chaplain in the military at the time. He had been at Normandy in June 1944 on the day of the slaughter, and he described that experience to Fred and some of the others in their dorm later that evening. He told how he went from soldier to soldier—many screaming, crying, dying, with bombs exploding all around—praying for them and speaking words of comfort.

Someone asked him, "With shells going off up and down the beach, everywhere, why did you do that?" He answered, "Because I am a minister."

In the course of the conversation someone asked him, "But didn't you ask them if they were Catholic or Protestant or Jew? I mean, if you are a minister . . ." Admiral Miller said, "If you are a minister, the only question you ask is, 'Can I help you?'"[9]

All Christians are ministers and the most important question ministers ask is not, "What do you believe?" but rather, "How can I help you?" When Mother Teresa ministered to the homeless, dying people of Calcutta she did not ask them what they believed. At that point in their lives, what they believed was irrelevant. She knew they were children of God, and her task was to help them trust and feel God's love through her kindness and attentiveness. She asked, "How can I help you?" And when they felt they were beyond help, beaten down so much by life that they did not feel worthy of help, she helped them all the more. She helped many, weighed down by the crushing burden of worthlessness, feel loved for the first time in their lives, making it possible for them to die with dignity.

Whatever spiritual disciplines we practice and find most helpful, either in personal retreat or corporately with others, if they do what they are supposed to do, we will be compelled into a life of service and compassion.

Going Deeper

1. Matthew 14:13 tells how Jesus withdrew by boat to a place of solitude upon hearing of the death of John the Baptist. Though his time of withdrawal was cut short by the presence of the crowd waiting on him when he reached the other side of the Sea of Galilee, still he was able to pray while on the boat. When Jesus saw the crowd, "he had compassion on them" (v. 14). Do you think the short time of solitude on the boat enabled Jesus to meet the crowd with compassion? Would it make a difference in your own capacity to love people and express compassion if you withdrew for short periods during the day to renew your spiritual energies?

2. Jesus was intimately connected to and immersed in the divine Spirit who provides spiritual energy and power for ministry, but Jesus needed time alone to nurture his own relationship with the Spirit. Some aspects of this relationship simply could not be developed while on the move or in the midst of ministry. Read Matthew 14:15-23. Why do you think Jesus dismissed the crowds and "went up the mountain by himself to pray"? If Jesus needed time alone with God, how much more do we?

3. There is no particular formula or method for replenishing one's spiritual energies through being alone with God. I find journaling revitalizing. Some people find that simply sitting in silence before God is what helps them. Others engage in centering prayer. There is no magic formula. We are each unique, and what I find beneficial may not be that helpful to you. Experiment and then share with your group or community what you have found that works for you.

Stages of Spiritual Struggle

Author Nikos Kazantzakis shared a great story about a monk. When Nikos was young, his mother was very religious and went to mass every day. His father was anti-religious, bitter toward religion, and Nikos was torn. When he was nineteen years old he decided to spend the summer at a monastery on one of the mountains in Greece. At this monastery there was a famous old monk called Father Makarios.

One day Nikos asked, "Father Makarios, do you still wrestle with the devil?" Father Makarios said, "No. I used to wrestle with the devil all the time. But now I have grown old and tired, and the devil has grown old and tired with me. So I leave him alone and he leaves me alone."

Nikos asked, "Then life is easy now?" Father Makarios responded: "Oh, no. Life is much harder now. For now I wrestle with God." Nikos exclaimed, "You wrestle with God and hope to win?" "No," said Father Makarios, "I wrestle with God and hope to lose."[10]

These two images—wrestling with the devil (I'm using this term metaphorically) and wrestling with God—represent two different aspects of spiritual struggle, perhaps, even two different stages of spiritual development.

For most of his ministry Jesus wrestles with the devil. Many of the struggles come from his provocation of the religious establishment. But on one occasion, his mother and brothers come to "take charge of him" because they think "he is out of his mind" (Mark 3:21, NIV). On another occasion, just after Jesus tells his disciples that he must be rejected, suffer, and die, Peter (as the representative for all the disciples) seeks to persuade him differently. Jesus responds, "Get behind me, Satan, for you are setting your mind not on divine things but human things" (Mark 8:33). Jesus faces many temptations aimed at diverting him from the way of the cross.

But when Jesus arrives at Gethsemane, he is now struggling with God. He tells his intimate circle of disciples, "I am deeply grieved, even unto death" (Mark 14:34), and he cries out to God asking that this cup of suffering be removed from him (Mark 14:36). Then, on the cross, Jesus cries, "My

God, my God, why have you forsaken me?" (Mark 15:34). I do not believe for one moment that God actually abandons Jesus on the cross, but Jesus, as the Son of Man, the human one, feels forsaken. Jesus is wrestling with God.

Our struggle with the devil is largely a struggle with the ego. The ego pulls us toward extremes: thinking too much of ourselves or thinking too little of ourselves. It's a struggle with the lust of the flesh, the lust of the eyes, and the pride of life (1 John 2:16). It's a struggle with the desire for power, possessions, and prestige. It is largely a struggle about how we will channel the great passions and energies of life.

Our struggle with God is largely about control and surrender to a greater purpose and cause. It's the struggle of surrender to the great mystery that supports, sustains, and transforms all reality. In some ways, our struggle with the devil is our resistance to the plowing of the field, while our struggle with God is our resistance to becoming the seed that grows in the field.

When we lose our struggle with God, then we are finally able to say, "Father, into your hands I commend my spirit." We come to know God at a more profound level of spiritual consciousness. When we lose our struggle with God, we know in our core being that we are intrinsically related to God and grounded in God, and that will be all we need to know. That will be enough.

Going Deeper

1. Why do we spend so much time protecting and promoting the ego? Why do we fear losing control? Can you name some areas in your life where you have denied God access?

2. Read and reflect on John 12:23-26. The reference to "eternal life" is a reference to an interactive, dynamic life in relationship and partnership with the divine, not simply life in heaven or life that lasts forever. The emphasis is more on the quality of life than it is on the quantity of life. It is God's life—the energy, vitality, and love of the divine Spirit—interacting with the human spirit. According to this passage, how does one access "eternal life"? What does it mean to "love one's life in the world" and "hate one's life in the world"? (Remember, this is spiritual/theological, symbolical/metaphorical language.)

3. Many great spiritual teachers tell us that only through surrender and relinquishment, only in letting go, do we discover who we really are. Do you think this is true? Why or why not?

Notes

[1]Joel Osteen, *Your Best Life Now: 7 Steps to Living at Your Full Potential* (New York: Warner Faith, 2004), 77.

[2]Ibid., 11-12.

[3]Trina Paulus, *Hope for the Flowers* (New York: Paulist Press, 1972), 76.

[4]Will D. Campbell, *Brother to a Dragonfly*, 25th anniv. ed. (New York: Continuum, 2007), 220-23.

[5]John Lewis, *Across that Bridge: Life Lessons and a Vision of Change* (New York: Hyperion, 2012), 105-106.

[6]Wendell Berry, *Jayber Crow* (Berkeley: Counterpoint, 2000), 295.

[7]Jürgen Moltmann, "Prisoner of Hope," in *Bread and Wine: Readings for Lent and Easter* (Farmington, PA: Plough Publishing House, 2003), 151.

[8]Sheila Fabricant, Dennis, and Matthew Linn, *Healing the Purpose of Your Life* (New York: Paulist Press, 1999), 42-43.

[9]Fred Craddock, *Craddock Stories*, ed. Mike Graves and Richard F. Ward (St. Louis: Chalice Press, 2001), 137.

[10]See Nikos Kasantzakis, *Report to Greco*, trans. Helen N. Kazantzakis (New York: Simon and Schuster, 1965), 222.

CHAPTER 6

The Upside-Down Kingdom
(Beatitudes)

What Possesses Us?

Jesus begins the Sermon on the Mount in Matthew's Gospel with the Beatitudes. (The teachings in Matthew 5-7 were no doubt uttered by Jesus in many different contexts; the biblical writer/redactor gathered them into this form.) The first beatitude is: "Blessed are the poor in spirit, for theirs is the kingdom of God" (Matt. 5:1). "Blessed" means something like "spiritually well-off" (the translation "happy" doesn't quite do it justice).

Luke's version simply reads: "Blessed are you who are poor, for yours is the kingdom of God" (6:20). Was Jesus referring to the materially poor or to a poverty of spirit before God? The Hebrew word that is behind the concept of "poor" conveys both of these meanings and, most likely, both would have been intended by Jesus.

In Luke's version there is a corresponding judgment: "But woe to you who are rich, for you have received your consolation" (6:24). How many sermons have you heard on that text? In Luke's Gospel, Jesus often speaks about the dangers of wealth. In one place he tells his disciples, "Sell your possessions, and give alms" (12:33). He instructs one would-be disciple who is very wealthy to give away all his possessions. When he is unable to comply, Jesus responds, "How hard it is for those who have wealth (this would include most of us who are reading this) to enter the kingdom of God" (18:24). In numerous contexts Jesus announces that when the kingdom is realized, the first now will then be last, and the last now will then be first.

If we take Jesus' words and actions in the Gospels seriously, it is clear that Jesus champions the cause of the poor (see Luke 4:17-19). There is no question that he exercises a preferential, perhaps even a prejudicial, compassion for the poor and the oppressed. Proponents of a gospel of prosperity and personal success will find no support for their cause in the words and deeds of Jesus of Nazareth.

I don't plan to give away all my possessions anytime soon. But the fact is: I may not be wealthy judged by American standards, but from a global perspective I am one of the "rich" (the haves) of the world. That means I am complicit to some degree in the disproportionate and inequitable distribution of the world's resources and come under the indictment of Jesus. It is good for me to cultivate a spirit of humility, generosity, and gratitude, but that does not remove the indictment.

American disciples of Jesus who take Jesus' life and words seriously must live with this tension, and "spiritualizing" all of Jesus' teaching on the subject is no solution. In the upside-down kingdom of God, the poor have the advantage, says Jesus.

If it is the role of the prophet "to comfort the afflicted and to afflict the comfortable," then Jesus is surely being the prophet in his teachings regarding possessions (afflicting us preachers as much as anyone). Keep in mind, too, that the call to relinquish possessions is also a call to relinquish the power, prestige, control, status, and honor that go with them. It's hardly ever just about money; it's what accompanies it.

When the rich man walks away sad, the disciples exclaim, "Who then can be saved?" (Meaning: Who can be spiritually well-off/whole/blessed?) Most of us would like Jesus to pat them on the back and say, "It will be okay." Instead Jesus says, "Well, it is impossible for human beings, but it is possible with God" (Luke 18:26-27).

There is a spiritual principle at work here: The less we are possessed by our possessions, the more God is able to possess us. The less hold (attachment) we have on our holdings, the more we are able to lay hold of the kingdom of God and find our joy in being companions of Christ and collaborators in his mission to realize God's dream for the world.

Going Deeper

1. Contemporary Christians face the temptation either to ignore, dismiss, or spiritualize Jesus' blessing on the poor and his warnings against wealth on the one hand, or to absolutize and literalize them on the other hand. How can we constructively and redemptively struggle with the tension this creates for modern American Christians?

2. What are the blessings of spiritual poverty? Is it possible for one to be wealthy and be characterized by spiritual poverty? Why or why not? What are the spiritual dangers of wealth?

3. In Luke 16:19-31 the rich man is condemned, not because he oppressed the poor (which is a dominant theme in the Hebrew prophetic writings), but because he did nothing to ease their burden. What can we do individually and as communities of faith to bridge the gap between the rich and poor, and to help alleviate the burden of those in poverty? Does the government in a democratic society have a part to play?

Living with Grief and Joy

A pilot practicing maneuvers in a jet fighter turned the controls for what he thought was a steep ascent and flew straight into the ground. He was unaware that he had been flying upside down.

Maybe that is true for many of us. We have been so conditioned by our culture that we don't know what is up or down when it comes to what is real and true. So when Jesus flips our world upside down in the Beatitudes, he is really turning it right side up.

The second beatitude in Jesus' Sermon on the Mount reads: "Blessed are those who mourn, for they will be comforted" (Matt. 5:4). Jesus is not giving his disciples timeless truths about the way the world is, for the world is not this way at all. In the world mourners often go uncomforted, but not in the kingdom of God.

This beatitude is based on Isaiah 61 where, in its broader context, the prophet is lamenting the desolation of the holy city and the spiritual and social condition of the people of God. Jesus reflects this spirit when he looks out over Jerusalem and cries, "Jerusalem, Jerusalem, the city that kills the prophets and stones those who are sent to it! How often have I desired to gather your children together as a hen gathers her brood under her wings, and you were not willing!" (Matt. 23:37).

Jesus mourns the spiritual and social state of his people, and yet he exudes an abundance of joy and peace. He, through God's Spirit, is able to hold the contradiction together. He is in great agony in Gethsemane, not only as he contemplates his own death, but perhaps more significantly, as he mourns the state of the covenant people whose leadership is mired in legalistic stipulations, aristocratic pride, and religious manipulation. Yet, in the shadow of the cross, he says to his disciples, "My peace I give to you . . . these things I have shared with you so that you may share my joy" (John 14:27, 15:11).

The late Clarence Jordan is a contemporary example of a disciple of Jesus living out this contradiction. He and his interracial farm community in Americus, Georgia, felt the prejudice, hate, and wrath of the powers that be. Their farm was boycotted and their people shot at. Their roadside market was destroyed by dynamite. In the middle of the violence against them their lives were in danger daily. Yet Jordan was known for his laughter, his clever wit, and his love for life. When the local and state powers boycotted their farm, this little community relied on friends throughout the country to get their pecans to market. Their slogan was: "Help us get the nuts out of Georgia."

This is the paradox: Even when we feel life diminished by the losses, suffering, and injustice of the human condition, we also discover life enhanced by the living Christ, immersing us in God's goodness and in God's dream for the world. Even as we mourn the poverty, oppression, and tragedies of life, as well as our own personal losses, we are sustained and strengthened by a deeper peace and joy.

Often, in our personal or communal experience, either sadness or joy has the upper hand. We sometimes journey through grief into joy, where the psalmist says that our mourning is turned into dancing. Our grief through our own personal losses and our ache at the evil and injustice in the world invites us to place our grief and hurt in larger hands. In one sense, there is no healing without woundedness, no growth without suffering, and no resurrection without death.

In Christ we are able, somehow, to experience both grief and joy simultaneously and live with the tension this creates. The Spirit enables us to hold these incongruities together. The living Christ invites us to share in both his suffering and joy.

Going Deeper

1. In what ways has your socialization into society resulted in obscuring, diluting, and clouding what is true, real, and just? Do you ever find yourself frustrated with Jesus' sayings to the point of becoming dismissive? Could that be because you are flying upside down?

2. The writer of James says, "My brothers and sisters, whenever you face trials of any kind, consider it nothing but joy" (Jas. 1:2). Paul says, "We also boast in our sufferings" (Rom. 5:3). Does this sound reasonable, logical, or even possible to you? How might it become possible for you to experience some degree of joy in the midst of your sufferings and trials?

3. I believe God is able to experience both deep sorrow and intense joy simultaneously. Being finite, usually sorrow or joy takes precedence in our experience. In times of great mourning or sorrow, how might we experience periods of joy? In times of great joy, how can we carve out periods to mourn with our suffering sisters and brothers?

Meekness Is Not Weakness

Jesus says, "Blessed are the meek, for they will inherit the earth" (Matt. 5:5). Inheriting the earth is another way of talking about the realization of God's kingdom in this world, not a heavenly world. That's not to say there is no heavenly world. I certainly believe there is, but once again Jesus' focus is on God's dream for this earth.

Meekness is not weakness. Jesus challenges the powers that be when he intentionally pushes the edges of religious respectability through his practice of an open table (inclusivity), identification with the marginalized, healing on the Sabbath, and intentional disregard for the holiness laws of clean and unclean.

Jesus does not, however, use his charismatic, spiritual power to control or coerce others to do his bidding. He empties himself of all selfish ambition as he lives and teaches forgiveness, nonviolence, and peacemaking.

The word translated "meek" in Jesus' beatitude could just as easily be translated "humble" or "gentle." Jesus says to his disciples, "Come to me, all you that are weary and are carrying heavy burdens, and I will give you rest. Take my yoke upon you, and learn from me; for I am gentle and humble in heart, and you will find rest for your souls" (Matt. 11:28-29). The word that is translated "gentle" in the above text is the same word that is translated "meek" in the beatitude. These are all related concepts.

The humility of Jesus does not in any way resemble timidity. It takes great courage, restraint, and spiritual strength for Jesus to confront the injustice and exclusivity of the powers that be, knowing full well that his challenge to the status quo would evoke the hate and animosity of the religious and political establishment, eventually bringing about his death.

What is authentic humility? *Rolling Stone* magazine interviewed Scott Weiland of the band, "The Stone Temple Pilots," after he had been released from prison, having served a term for drug possession. In the interview he kept using the word "humility." The reporter asked him to define the term. Scott Weiland said, "It's not me thinking less of myself. It's me thinking of myself less."

In my opinion, too many Christians have overemphasized the biblical story of the fall at the expense of the story of creation. Certainly we are all flawed and broken. We have a selfish bent and a strong propensity to seek and misuse worldly power. But that doesn't mean we are "no good" or "no account." Humility is not someone saying, "I am a wretch; I am a worm." It is not debasement, self-contempt, or self-hate.

We are created in God's image. The biblical story of redemption is rooted in our worth and value. Every person is a child of God, no matter how flawed or sinful. We are each worth redeeming, and I believe, in God's time (it will take much longer with some than others) everyone will be redeemed. I believe that the death and resurrection of Jesus serve as the ultimate demonstration that divine love will one day triumph, transforming the most evil persons into persons who will finally learn how to be good, merciful, and just. I believe that God will eventually get what God wants and that every person—every one of God's children, every one of God's free creatures—will see the light, repent of all the evil that the light exposes, and pursue the path that leads to redemption. Then, love will triumph.

Humility is not thinking less of myself but thinking of myself less, so I can think more of others and serve others. It is being less self-absorbed, so I can be more other-centered. It is being less preoccupied with my ego desires, so I can seek first the kingdom of God, nurture caring relationships, and work for the good of the planet.

Meekness is not weakness, humility is not timidity, and Jesus' relinquishment of worldly power is not powerlessness. In God's upside-down kingdom, the powerbrokers of the world will find themselves last, and the meek will inherit the earth.

Going Deeper

1. In what ways do you think meekness/humility is a misunderstood concept in Western culture?

2. I do not believe Jesus was as tempted by evil as he was tempted by good. Jesus faced the temptation to employ the methods of worldly power to accomplish the work of the kingdom of God. His refusal to yield to that temptation makes clear that, from Jesus' perspective, the end does not justify the use of manipulative or coercive power. Yet Jesus demonstrated great spiritual power in his confrontation with evil (see Mark 1:21-28) and in his constant clash and confrontation with the religious establishment. Do you think Jesus showed humility in the exercise of such power and authority? Can one be both humble and confrontational (perhaps even provocative) at the same time?

3. Philip Gulley, in a message on humility, quoted Monica Baldwin, a nun who lived in an isolated convent for twenty-eight years. After only a few years in the convent, she began to think she had made a mistake. Writing in her journal, she said, "I am no more fitted to be a nun than I am an acrobat." When she finally left the convent, she wrote about her experiences. In one place she wrote, "What makes humility so desirable is the marvelous thing it does to us; it creates in us a capacity for the closest possible intimacy with God."[1] Why is this true?

Hungering For Justice

Some years ago popular speaker and author Tony Campolo helped initiate a master's program at Eastern College that trains students to enter Third World countries, as well as impoverished sections of American cites, with the express purpose of starting small businesses and cottage industries with the poor. Campolo was once part of such a micro enterprise in the Dominican Republic that produced durable footwear out of discarded automobile tires.

Campolo declared, "When we talk about Jesus, we make it clear that he is not just interested in our well-being in the afterlife. He is a Savior who is at work in the world today trying to save the world from what it is, and make it into a place where people can live together with dignity."[2] This, I believe, is what Jesus has in mind when he says, "Blessed are those who hunger and thirst for righteousness, for they will be filled" (Matt. 5:6).

The word translated "righteousness" can also be translated "justice." Justice in the Hebrew-Christian tradition differs significantly from what many folks today mean when they use the term. Justice, as employed by the prophets and by Jesus, does not mean "getting what one deserves." According to Old Testament scholar Walter Brueggemann, the meaning of "justice/righteousness" is principally about actions that sustain and improve community well-being, particularly those that show special attentiveness to the poor and needy.[3] The Hebrew prophets rail against religious and political leaders who spurn justice, but yet are very pious and religious (see Amos 5:21-24).

Restorative justice is not about what is legal; rather, it concerns what is good, fair, gracious, and just. It's committed to the dignity of all people and to eliminating the causes of oppression, poverty, and injustice. Its focus is the common good, not private interest. It's centered on God's kingdom on earth, not the afterlife. (We need not worry about or concern ourselves with the afterlife, because our gracious heavenly father/mother will take good care of all of us.)

The late social prophet William Sloan Coffin noted that public good does not necessarily follow on the heels of private virtue. A person's moral character in and of itself is insufficient to serve the cause of justice. It takes great courage to challenge the status quo and speak truth to power. Real virtue is bound to the pursuit of justice—the well-being and life enhancement of the community. Without this quality our religion fails and falls under the judgment of God.

Social justice is not the same thing as acts of personal and communal charity for the poor and disadvantaged. The following story highlights the difference.

Once there was a town built just beyond the bend of a large river. One day some of the children from the town were playing beside the river when they noticed three bodies floating in the water. They ran for help and the townsfolk quickly pulled the bodies out of the river.

One person was dead, so they buried that one. One was alive, but very sick, so they put that person in the hospital. The third turned out to be a healthy child, who they placed with a family that cared for the child and took the child to school.

From that day forward, a number of bodies came floating down the river and every day, the good people of the town would pull them out and tend to them—taking the sick to the hospital, placing children with families, and burying those who were dead.

This went on for years. Each week brought its quota of bodies, and the townsfolk not only came to expect a number of bodies each week, but also developed more elaborate systems for picking them out of the river and tending to them. Some even gave up their jobs so they could devote themselves to this work full time. The townspeople began to even feel a certain healthy pride in their generosity and care for them.

However, during all those years and despite all their generosity, no one thought to go up the river, beyond the bend that hid from sight what was above them, and find out why all those bodies kept floating down the river.

Herein is the difference between private charity and social justice, between doing acts of mercy and confronting systems of injustice. Private charity responds to the needs of the homeless and the poor, but social justice tries to get at the reasons why there are homeless and poor people in the first place and offer constructive solutions.

While charity is about giving a hungry person some bread, social justice is about trying to change the system so that no one has excess bread while some have none. Charity is about helping the victims of war, while social justice is about peacemaking and eliminating the conditions that lead to war.

Social justice tackles such issues as poverty, inequality, war, racism, sexism, heath care, violence, immigration, and the environment. It takes on huge, blind economic, political, social, and religious systems that deprive some even as they unduly privilege others—systems in which we are all complicit.

It is easy to understand why many present-day Christians have relinquished this responsibility and redefined the gospel so that it is not about social justice at all. Social justice is challenging, difficult, risky work.

And yet the church has a history of engaging in social justice. In our country Christians played a large part in the acquisition of voting rights for women, in the overthrow of slavery, in the abolishment of segregation laws and the passing of civil rights legislation, and in the establishment of rights for and improving the conditions of the most vulnerable in our courts, prisons, schools, and everywhere else. There is a movement today among the more progressive mainline and evangelical Christians to make social justice an integral and nonnegotiable part of what it means to live the gospel.

The challenge we face is the same challenge Jesus faced in preaching good news to the poor, proclaiming freedom to the captives, giving sight to the blind (helping people become aware of their responsibility), and liberating the oppressed (Luke 4:18). The "powers that be" will seek to stifle our efforts. Will we settle for the status quo, or will we live the gospel of Jesus?

Without a hunger and thirst for social justice, the church is not the church. For the church to be what Jesus envisioned—an outpost for God's kingdom on earth—the church must cultivate a hunger and thirst for restorative justice.

Going Deeper

1. The more we are tied to and entrenched within systems of injustice, whether they are economic, political, social, or religious, the more difficult it is to question and challenge these systems. It's much easier to remain blind to the truth, or worse, call evil good and then find Scripture, church, and religious teachings to bless our idolatries. In what ways are you complicit in systems of injustice?

2. Read and reflect on Isaiah 1:1-20. How does Isaiah describe the people depicted in this passage? In what ways had they forsaken the Lord? What is Isaiah's prescription for their spiritual sickness?

3. William Sloan Coffin said: "There are three kinds of patriots, two bad, one good. The bad ones are the uncritical lovers and loveless critics. Good patriots carry on a lover's quarrel with their country, a reflection of God's lover's quarrel with the world."[4] What kind of patriot are you? What sort of lover's quarrels are you having with your country (political establishment) and your church (religious establishment) right now? What quarrels should you be having?

Swimming in God's Mercy

Jesus says, "Blessed are the merciful, for they will receive mercy" (Matt. 5:7). One biblical scholar has paraphrased this as "compassion in action." It's not just feeling sympathy or empathy for others, though these elements are included; it's doing something for them. When the blind cry out to Jesus, "Son of David, have mercy on us," they are not asking for sympathy or even empathy; they want healing (see Matt. 20:29-34).

Justice and mercy go hand in hand. Isaiah asks, "What kind of fast is acceptable to the Lord?" (Isa. 58:5). The prophet says, "Is this not the fast that I choose: to loose the bonds of injustice, to undo the thongs of the yoke, to let the oppressed go free, to break every yoke? Is it not to share your bread with the hungry, and bring the homeless poor into your house; when you see the naked, to cover them, and not to hide yourself from your own kin? (vv. 6-7). To turn away from the needy is not only to deny their humanity, but also to deny our own; it is to forfeit what it means to be human.

Bob Riley, a conservative winner of the Friend of Taxpayers Award several years running, was elected governor of Alabama in 2002. He discovered that the tax code had not been changed since 1901. He pointed out that the wealthiest Alabamians paid three percent of their income in taxes and the poorest up to twelve percent. Out-of-state timber companies paid only $1.25 per acre in property taxes. Alabama was third from the bottom of all states in total taxes, and almost all of that came from sales taxes, which of course, are paid in higher proportion by people who need to spend most of their income on basic needs.

So Riley proposed a tax hike, partly to dig the state out of its fiscal crisis and partly to bring more money into the state's school system. He argued that it was their Christian responsibility to attend to the needs of the poor more carefully. This meant that wealthy Alabamians would have to pay more taxes.

The leader of the Christian Coalition of Alabama spearheaded the opposition. He said, "You'll find most Alabamians have got a charitable heart. They just don't want it coming out of their pockets." The law was defeated and the schools remained underfunded. The leader of the Christian Coalition should read the prophets and the Gospels.

Jesus upsets many of the religious leaders of his day because he criticizes and rebukes them for their lack of mercy. Twice in Matthew's Gospel Jesus quotes Hosea 6:6 where God says to his people, "For I desire steadfast love and not sacrifice, the knowledge of God rather than burnt offerings." The ritual sacrificing of animals was a key element in Israel's early religious worship and development. It's all useless and empty, says Jesus, without mercy, without compassion in action.

My favorite Old Testament story is the story of Jonah, a prophet who is told by God to go to Nineveh to warn the people about God's judgment. He doesn't want to go, because he knows that if they listen and humble themselves before God and turn from their evil ways, God will show mercy.

So Jonah heads off in the opposite direction, but God gets him turned around. He figures that since he is a prophet, he had better do what God says. So Jonah goes to Nineveh, but he is not happy about it. When the people of Nineveh repent and God shows mercy, Jonah is angry. Jonah wants mercy for *his* people, but not for the people of Nineveh—not the enemy. Jonah resents God's inclusive mercy. The story ends with Jonah sitting in the hot sun, stewing.

Of course, the great irony in the story is the same irony we see time and time again in the history of redemption, and that we see with Jesus and the religious leaders. The very ones who should be champions and advocates of God's mercy resist it, and those you would think would be most resistant welcome it, embrace it, and let it change them.

Disciples of Jesus are called to swim in the ocean of God's mercy and be conduits through which that mercy can flow to all people, even the enemy. God's mercy is inexhaustible. We can draw from the wellspring of God's mercy again and again. But here's the catch: We can't keep it for ourselves—for our group, people, or nation. We have to give it away. "Blessed are the merciful, for they will be shown mercy."

Going Deeper

1. There are some people like Jonah who have trouble showing mercy to those outside their group, but then, there are still others who have trouble showing mercy to themselves. This often finds expression in neurotic guilt, self-hate, shame, and depression. Spiritual writer and retreat leader Brennan Manning has confessed to this tendency. He said that the key to overcoming self-condemnation is through unshakable trust in the compassion and mercy of Christ. Do you have unshakable trust in the compassion and mercy of Christ? How can you nurture such trust?

2. Read Matthew 9:10-13 and 12:1-8. What does, "I desire mercy, not sacrifice" mean in these stories/contexts?

3. Sometimes mercy is demonstrated not only by what we do, but also through what we refrain from doing. Forgiveness is an act of mercy. When we forgive a debt or an offense, absorbing the hurt, debt, or offense in ourselves, we are showing mercy. For many of us, forgiveness is a difficult process. What makes forgiveness so hard?

Pursuing God's New World

Jesus says, "Blessed are the pure in heart, for they will see God" (Matt. 5:8). Many people think this has something to do with how we feel, because so often in our culture we use the word "heart" to stand for our emotions or feelings. We speak of deep emotion as breaking our hearts. So naturally we think of "pure in heart" as a reference to those who are sincere in their devotion to God. The idea of sincerity is certainly included, but that is not Jesus' primary meaning.

In its scriptural usage, the "heart" certainly includes the emotions, but it is actually much broader. It represents the whole realm of human consciousness and activity. The heart is a symbol for what we are in ourselves, and stands for the source of all our aspirations, dreams, intentions, attitudes, and reactions. Jesus is saying, "Blessed are those who have a pure source of life in them."

In Matthew 6:22-23, immediately following a reference to the "heart" in verse 21, Matthew applies Jesus' reference to "the eye" as an image of the heart. The eye is to the body what the heart is to all of life. When the "eye is healthy," then "the whole body is full of light." But when the "eye is unhealthy," then the "whole body is full of darkness." Jesus is saying that the condition of the heart determines whether we are blind or can "see"; whether our lives are full of goodness or evil.

The reference to purity in this beatitude can just as easily be misunderstood as the reference to the heart. One of Søren Kierkegaard's famous lines (also the title of the book) was "Purity of heart is to will one thing." A person who is "pure in heart" is undivided or single-minded in his or her intention.

There's a wonderful scene in the movie *City Slickers* where Curly (Jack Palance), the tough-as-nails, wise-to-the-ways-of-the-world trail boss, asked Mitch (Billy Crystal) if he wanted to know the secret of life. Curly said, "It's this," holding up his index finger. Mitch retorted, "The secret of life is your finger." Curly, never batting an eye said, "It's one thing. The secret of life is pursuing one thing."

The Quaker mystic Thomas Kelly, in his spiritual classic, *A Testament of Devotion*, wrote about how difficult it is for Westerners to live out of a controlling center because we are so divided and unskilled in the inner life. Our tendency, said Kelly, is to try to be several selves at once, without all our selves being organized by a single, mastering life within. Our lives are divided into the civic self, the parental self, the financial self, the religious self, the social self, the professional self—any number of selves, each wanting its piece of the pie.[5] But we have no center around which these revolve to keep them balanced and integrated.

According to Jesus, the one thing his disciples are called to pursue is the kingdom of God. In a context where Jesus tells his disciples not to be anxious about how they appear to others, nor about their daily needs (what they will eat, drink, and wear), he says, "But strive first for the kingdom of God and his righteousness (justice), and all these will be given to you as well" (Matt. 6:33). In other words, *everything* else in life will find its place around life's central priority—the kingdom of God.

To live to eat and drink and dress, to pursue meaning in how we appear to others and in our temporal security, is to invite anxiety into our lives (see Matt. 6:25-32). It's a sure recipe for frustration and depression. Stress-filled anxiety stems from a divided life. The way out, the way to be liberated from greed, anger, and despair is by making the kingdom of God (which is oriented around God's restorative justice) the integrating center, the singleness of intent that orients everything else. Doing this does not mean that we neglect other relationships and responsibilities; rather, we can now give them their proper attention and value as we put them in a kingdom perspective.

Living out of this center—developing a singleness of intention oriented around God's kingdom—does not add to the complexity of our lives; it has the opposite effect. Instead of adding stress and strain and creating more burden and anxiety, it actually frees us from such things. It brings our lives together around the one thing, the integrating reality. This is why the spiritual masters call this kind of life a life of simplicity.

Jesus promises that all who are so integrated, balanced, and intentional in pursuing God's new world "will see God." Throughout the Gospels "seeing" is a way of talking about understanding, perceiving, and grasping the truth in a transformative way. It's the capacity to see through our many deceptions, illusions, and subtle lies, and recognize what is real, true, just, and good. No one will ever see the essence of God, but we can see the beauty and goodness of God in one another, in life's experiences, and in creation.

As we give ourselves to the healing, wholeness, and well-being of others, we will find our own redemption. We most certainly will become "more" and "better" than what we are now when we truly "see" God in ourselves, others, and the world.

Going Deeper

1. Søren Kierkegaard compared the state of Christianity in his day with taking a half dose of medicine. Imagine a kind of medicine that possesses in full dosage a laxative effect, but in a half dose a constipating effect. Suppose someone is suffering from constipation. But perhaps because there is not enough for a full dose or because it is feared that such a large amount might be too much, the person suffering from constipation is given a half-dose rather than a full dose. All it does is make the condition worse.[6] Have you ever experienced religious practice as "making the condition worse," or like getting a vaccine that made you immune to the real thing? What religious practices will help you find an integrating center and singleness of focus around the kingdom of God?

2. Richard Rohr has contended that spirituality and faith have more to do with subtraction, with becoming less, than with addition, with becoming more (less is more). He particularly emphasized the need to let go of the guilt of the past and the fear of the future in order to live fully in the now.[7] What steps can you take to simplify your life so that you can live more fully in the now instead of being shackled with the burdens of the past and the worries of the future?

3. What does Mark 7:1-23 teach about real holiness/purity?

Called To Be Peacemakers

Jesus says, "Blessed are the peacemakers, for they will be called the children of God" (Matt. 5:9). This beatitude is not about those who enjoy the fruits of peace, but those who give themselves to the difficult and challenging work of making peace between individuals, families, groups, and nations.

An excellent contemporary example is Nelson Mandela. When he assumed the reins of power in South Africa, he refused to be bitter toward his enemies. After twenty-seven years of imprisonment, he refrained from any form of vindictiveness and called on all races to work together to heal the nation.

At the core of all peacemaking is a basic commitment to nonviolence. Only nonviolence can break the cycle of violence and open a door for peace. Violence can never stop violence because its very success leads others to imitate it. It's ironic, but violence can be the most dangerous when it succeeds.

However successful we are in our war against terror, it will not put an end to terrorism. Governments face hard decisions, but whenever violence is met with violence it causes hate and animosity to escalate. Every terrorist we kill, and particularly every civilian that gets caught or killed in the crossfire, becomes a cause for recruitment to the terrorist agenda and increases their hatred.

Our society is so saturated and prone toward violence that people find it hard to believe in anything else. Many people tend to trust violence. Biblical support is easy to marshal. One can find any number of divinely sanctioned expressions of violence in the Bible, even divinely commissioned genocide. Jesus, however, while treating his sacred Scriptures and traditions with great respect, does not blindly accept everything in the Bible hook, line, and sinker.

Jesus exposes the lie and deception of so-called "redemptive violence" when he grounds his teaching to love our enemies on the very nature and character of God (Matt. 5:43-48). Jesus embodies a life of nonviolence through what he teaches, how he lives, and especially in the way and manner in which he dies. This is why the cross becomes the foundational symbol and expression of the gospel of peace. Jesus bears the cruelty, animosity, and violence of the political and religious powers without returning them.

Peacemaking through nonviolence, however, does not involve being a "doormat." In Matthew 5:38-42, Jesus mentions some examples of how his followers could take nonviolent direct action against the oppressive powers of his day. When Jesus says, "Do not resist an evil person" he is not telling them to be completely passive. The phrase actually means, "Do not violently resist an evil person." Jesus enumerates some ways to creatively resist without being violent, such as standing one's ground to be hit again, refusing to succumb to the humiliation of being slapped, or by carrying a soldier's bag an additional mile, refusing to put it down (according to Roman law, a soldier could only require a non-citizen of Rome to carry it one mile). To resist nonviolently in these ways requires great moral strength and spiritual courage.

Peacemaking through nonviolence does not mean conflict avoidance. There are numerous times in the Gospels when Jesus acts in defiance of the religious authorities, thus provoking conflict. Nonviolent peacemaking will sometimes elicit and provoke conflict as a way of exposing prejudice and injustice. This was a common strategy of the civil rights marchers.

It is not by accident that the final beatitude following the blessing on peacemakers is, "Blessed are those who are persecuted for righteousness sake, for theirs is the kingdom of heaven" (Matt. 5:10). Peacemakers can expect to be persecuted, but they are always looking for creative alternatives to violence. There may be times in self-defense that we have to resort to force, but disciples of Jesus should always be looking for creative ways to diffuse violence and make peace, even when it involves bearing the hate without returning it—the way Jesus did on the cross.

Biblical scholar Walter Wink has noted a number of examples where nonviolence has worked. Bulgaria's Orthodox Bishop Kiril told Nazi authorities that if they attempted to deport Bulgarian Jews to concentration camps, he himself would lead a campaign of civil disobedience, lying down on the railroad tracks in front of the trains. Thousands of Bulgarian Jews and non-Jews resisted all collaboration with Nazi decrees. They marched in mass street demonstrations and sent a flood of letters and telegrams to authorities protesting all anti-Jewish measures. Bulgarian clergy and laity hid Jews. Christian ministers accepted large numbers of Jewish "converts," making it clear that this was a trick to evade arrest and that they would not consider their "vows" binding. All of Bulgaria's Jewish citizens were saved from the Nazi death camps through these nonviolent actions.

Finland saved all but six of its Jewish citizens from death camps through nonmilitary means. The Norwegian underground helped nine hundred Jews flee to safety in Sweden. In Italy, a large percentage of Jews survived because officials and citizens sabotaged efforts to hand them over to the Germans.[8]

Of course there are some situations that are simply tragic, where nothing we can conceive of doing will help. But as disciples of Jesus we must look for nonviolent alternatives. Our capacity to find nonviolent alternatives in times of crisis will depend, to some degree, on whether we practice nonviolent responses in our everyday interactions.

Blessed are the peacemakers, for they will be called children of God. Why? Because we are never more like God than when we act in forgiveness and seek nonviolent alternatives to hate and violence.

Going Deeper

1. Reflect on the question posed by U.S. Congressman and former civil rights leader John Lewis: "What is it about our psyche or makeup as human beings that invites us to project our fear upon one another, justify abuse to relieve our own anxieties, and then demonize the object of our ridicule?"[9]

2. It takes great inner resolve and spiritual maturity to engage in the pursuit of justice and peace in redemptive ways. What are the dangers of engaging in social activism without the necessary spiritual disciplines and resources to sustain us in the struggle?

3. Do you think human rights are at the heart of the gospel? Why or why not?

Notes

[1]Philip Gulley, "The Qualities of the Spiritual Life (Humility)," philipgulley.org, 5.

[2]Tony Campolo, *Let Me Tell You a Story: Life Lessons from Unexpected Places and Unlikely People* (Waco: W Publishing Group, 2000), 125-26.

[3]Walter Brueggemann, *Reverberations of Faith: A Theological Handbook of Old Testament Themes* (Louisville: Westminster John Knox Press, 2002), 177.

[4]William Sloan Coffin, *Credo* (Louisville: Westminster John Knox Press, 2004), 84.

[5]Thomas R. Kelly, *A Testament of Devotion* (New York: HarperSanFrancisco, 1992), 93.

[6]Søren Kiergegaard, *Provocations: Spiritual Writings of Kierkegaard*, comp./ed. Charles E. Moore (Farmington, PA: Plough Publishing Co., 1999), 16-18.

[7]Richard Rohr, *Simplicity: The Freedom of Letting Go*, rev. ed. (New York: Crossroad Publishing Co., 2003), 171.

[8]Walter Wink, *The Powers That Be: Theology for a New Millennium* (New York: Doubleday, 1998), 152.

[9]John Lewis, *Across That Bridge: Life Lessons and a Vision for Change* (New York: Hyperion Books, 2012), 120-21.

Recommended Reading

The following list is not in any way intended to be exhaustive. These are all books that I have personally read and found helpful in expounding progressive Christian themes. Deserving of special mention are two authors: Richard Rohr, for the profound way his writings have mentored me in the spiritual life, and Marcus Borg, whose writings were instrumental in prompting me to think of Jesus in new ways.

Autry, James A. *Looking Around for God: The Oddly Reverent Observations of an Unconventional Christian.* Macon, GA: Smyth & Helwys, 2007.

Baker, Sharon L. *Razing Hell: Rethinking Everything You've Been Taught about God's Wrath and Judgment.* Louisville: Westminster John Knox Press, 2010.

Bass, Diana Butler. *Christianity after Religion: The End of the Church and the Birth of a New Spiritual Awakening.* New York: HarperOne, 2012.

_____. *Christianity for the Rest of Us.* New York: HarperSanFrancisco, 2006.

Bawer, Bruce. *Stealing Jesus: How Fundamentalism Betrays Christianity.* New York: Three Rivers Press, 1997.

Bell, Rob. *Love Wins: A Book about Heaven, Hell, and the Fate of Every Person Who Ever Lived.* New York: HarperOne, 2011.

_____. *Velvet Elvis: Repainting the Christian Faith.* Grand Rapids: Zondervan, 2005.

Bell, Rob and Don Golden. *Jesus Wants to Save Christians: A Manifesto for the Church in Exile.* Grand Rapids: Zondervan, 2008.

Borg, Marcus J. *Jesus: A New Vision.* New York: HarperSanFrancisco, 1987.

_____. *Jesus: Uncovering the Life, Teachings, and Relevance of a Religious Revolutionary.* New York: HarperSanFrancisco, 2006.

_____. *Meeting Jesus Again for the First Time: The Historical Jesus & the Heart of Contemporary Faith.* New York: HarperSanFrancisco, 1994.

_____. *Speaking Christian: Why Christian Words Have Lost Their Meaning and Power—And How They Can Be Restored.* New York: HarperOne, 2011.

_____. *The Heart of Christianity: Rediscovering a Life of Faith*. New York: HarperSanFrancisco, 2003.

Borg, Marcus J. and John Dominic Crossan. *The First Paul: Reclaiming the Radical Visionary Behind the Church's Conservative Icon*. New York: HarperOne, 2009.

Borg, Marcus J. and N. T. Wright, *The Meaning of Jesus: Two Visions*. New York: HarperSanFrancisco, 1999.

Bourgeault, Cynthia. *The Wisdom Jesus: Transforming Heart and Mind—a New Perspective on Christ and His Message*. Boston: Shambhala, 2008.

Brueggemann, Walter. *Reverberations of Faith: A Theological Handbook of Old Testament Themes*. Louisville: Westminster John Knox Press, 2002.

Buechner, Frederick. *Wishful Thinking: A Seeker's ABC*. New York: HarperOne, 1993.

Burke, Spencer and Barry Taylor. *A Heretic's Guide to Eternity*. San Francisco: Jossey-Bass, 2006.

Burklo, Jim. *Open Christianity: Home by Another Road*. Scotts Valley, CA: Rising Star Press, 2000.

Campbell, Will D. *Brother to a Dragonfly*. 25th anniv. ed. New York: Continuum, 2007.

Chisttister, Joan. *Called to Question: A Spiritual Memoir*. Lanham, MD: Sheed & Ward, 2004.

Cobb, Jr., John B. *Process Perspective: Frequently Asked Questions about Process Theology*. Edited by Jeanyne B. Slettom. St. Louis: Chalice Press, 2003.

Coffin, William Sloan. *Credo*. Louisville: Westminster John Knox Press, 2004.

_____. *Letters to a Young Doubter*. Louisville: Westminster John Knox Press, 2005.

Cornwall, Robert D. *Faith in the Public Square*. Gonzales, FL: Energion Publications, 2012.

Cox, Harvey. *When Jesus Came to Harvard: Making Moral Choices Today*. New York: Houghton Mifflin Co., 2004.

_____. *The Future of Faith*. New York: HarperOne, 2009.

Crossan, John Dominic. *God and Empire: Jesus Against Rome, Then and Now*. New York: HarperOne, 2007.

_____. *The Greatest Prayer: Rediscovering the Revolutionary Message of the Lord's Prayer*. New York: HarperOne, 2010.

Dark, David. *The Sacredness of Questioning Everything*. Grand Rapids: Zondervan, 2009.

Dowd, Michael. *Thank God for Evolution: How the Marriage of Science and Religion Will Transform Your Life and World*. Canada: Council Oak Books, 2001.

Dunn, James D. G. *Jesus' Call to Discipleship*, Understanding Jesus Today series. Cambridge: Cambridge University Press, 1992.

Elnes, Eric. *The Phoenix Affirmations: A New Vision for the Future of Christianity*. San Francisco: Jossey-Bass, 2006.

Epperly, Bruce G. *Holy Adventure: 41 Days of Audacious Living*. Nashville: Upper Room Books, 2008.

Felten, David M. and Jeff Procter-Murphy. *Living the Questions: The Wisdom of Progressive Christianity*. New York: HarperOne, 2012.

Furnish, Victor Paul. *The Moral Teaching of Paul: Selected Issues*. 2nd ed. Nashville: Abingdon Press, 1985.

Gomes, Peter J. *The Good Book: Reading the Bible with Mind and Heart*. New York: William Morrow, 1996.

_____. *The Scandalous Gospel of Jesus: What's So Good about the Good News?* New York: HarperCollins, 2007.

Green, Joel B., and Mark D. Baker. *Recovering the Scandal of the Cross: Atonement in New Testament & Contemporary Contexts*. Downers Grove, IL: InterVarsity Press, 2000.

Gulley, Philip. *If the Church Were Christian: Rediscovering the Values of Jesus.* New York: HarperOne, 2010.

_____. *The Evolution of Faith: How God is Creating a Better Christianity.* New York: HarperOne, 2011.

Gulley, Philip and James Mulholland. *If Grace Is True: Why God Will Save Every Person.* New York: HarperSanFrancisco, 2003.

_____. *If God Is Love: Rediscovering Grace in an Ungracious World.* New York: HarperSanFrancisco, 2004.

Hall, John Douglas. *The Cross in Our Context: Jesus and the Suffering World.* Minneapolis: Fortress Press, 2003.

Heschel, Abraham Joshua. *The Prophets.* New York: Harper and Row, 1962.

Hill, Craig C. In *God's Time: The Bible and the Future.* Grand Rapids / Cambridge: Eerdmans Publishing Co., 2002.

Horsley, Richard A. *Jesus and Empire: The Kingdom of God and the New World Disorder.* Minneapolis: Fortress Press, 2003.

Johnson, Elizabeth A. *Quest for the Living God: Mapping Frontiers in the Theology of God.* New York: Continuum, 2008.

Jones, Alan. *Reimagining Christianity: Reconnect Your Spirit without Disconnecting Your Mind.* Hoboken, NJ: John Wiley & Sons, 2005.

Jones, L. Gregory. *Embodying Forgiveness: A Theological Analysis.* Grand Rapids: Eerdmans Publishing Co., 1995.

Jones, Tony. *The New Christians: Dispatches from the Emergent Frontier.* San Francisco: Jossey-Bass, 2008.

Jordan, Clarence. *Essential Writings: Modern Spiritual Masters Series.* Maryknoll, NY: Orbis Books, 2003.

_____. *The Substance of Faith: And Other Cotton Patch Sermons.* Edited by Dallas Lee. Eugene, OR: Cascade Books, 2005.

Kidd, Sue Monk. *When the Heart Waits: Spiritual Direction for Life's Sacred Questions.* New York: HarperSanFrancisco, 1990.

Kimball, Charles. *When Religion Becomes Evil: Five Warning Signs.* New York: HarperSanFrancisco, 2002.

Knitter, Paul F. *Introducing Theologies of Religion.* Maryknoll, NY: Orbis Books, 2002.

Küng, Hans. *On Being a Christian.* Translated by Edward Quinn. New York: Doubleday, 1976.

Levine, Amy-Jill. *The Misunderstood Jew: The Church and the Scandal of the Jewish Jesus.* New York: HarperCollins, 2006.

Linn, Dennis, Sheila Fabricant Linn, and Matthew Linn. *Good Goats: Healing Our Image of God.* New York: Paulist Press, 1995.

_____. *Understanding Difficult Scriptures in a Healing Way.* New York: Paulist Press, 2001.

McLaren, Brian D. *A New Kind of Christianity: Ten Questions That Are Transforming the Faith.* New York: HarperOne, 2010.

_____. *Everything Must Change: Jesus, Global Crises, and a Revolution of Hope.* Nashville: Thomas Nelson, 2007.

_____. *Naked Spirituality: A Life with God in 12 Simple Words.* New York: HarperOne, 2011.

McSwain, Steve. *The Enoch Factor: The Sacred Art of Knowing God.* Macon, GA: Smyth & Helwys, 2010.

Mesle, C. Robert. *Process Theology: A Basic Introduction.* St. Louis: Chalice Press, 1993.

Moltmann, Jürgen. *In the End—The Beginning: The Life of Hope.* Translated by Margaret Kohl. Minneapolis: Fortress Press, 2004.

Nolan, Albert. *Jesus Before Christianity,* 25th anniv. ed. Maryknoll, NY: Orbis Books, 2001

_____. *Jesus Today: A Spirituality of Radical Freedom.* Maryknoll, NY: Orbis Books, 2008.

Nouwen, Henri J. M. *Finding My Way Home: Pathways to Life and the Spirit.* New York: Crossroad Publishing Co., 2001.

_____. *Here and Now: Living in the Spirit.* New York: Crossroad Publishing Co., 1994.

_____. *Life of the Beloved: Spiritual Living in a Secular World.* 10th anniv. ed. New York: Crossroad Publishing Co., 1992.

_____. *Making All Things New: An Invitation to the Spiritual Life.* New York: HarperCollins, 1981.

_____. *The Only Necessary Thing: Living a Prayerful Life.* Compiled and edited by Wendy Wilson Greer. New York: Crossroad Publishing Co., 1999.

_____. *The Return of the Prodigal Son: A Story of Homecoming.* New York: Doubleday, 1992.

Oord, Thomas Jay. *The Nature of Love: A Theology.* St. Louis: Chalice Press, 2010.

Palmer, Parker J. *Let Your Life Speak: Listening for the Voice of Vocation.* San Francisco: Jossey-Bass, 2000.

_____. *The Active Life: A Spirituality of Work, Creativity, and Caring.* San Francisco: Jossey-Bass, 1990.

Pregeant, Russell. *Reading the Bible for All the Wrong Reasons.* Minneapolis: Fortress Press, 2011.

Queen, Chuck. *A Faith Worth Living: The Dynamics of an Inclusive Gospel.* Eugene, OR: Resource Publications, 2011.

_____. *Shimmers of Light: Spiritual Reflections for the Christmas Season.* Eugene, OR: Resource Publications, 2011.

_____. *The Good News According to Jesus: A New Kind of Christianity for a New Kind of Christian.* Macon, GA: Smyth & Helwys, 2009.

_____. *Why Call Friday Good: Spiritual Reflections for Lent and Holy Week.* Eugene, OR: Resource Publications, 2012.

Rohr, Richard. *A Lever and a Place to Stand: The Contemplative Stance, The Active Prayer.* Mahwah, NJ: HiddenSpring, 2011.

_____. *Everything Belongs: The Gift of Contemplative Prayer.* New York: Crossroad Publishing Co., 2003.

_____. *Falling Upward: A Spirituality for the Two Halves of Life.* San Francisco: Jossey-Bass, 2011.

_____. *Immortal Diamond: The Search for Our True Self.* San Francisco: Jossey-Bass, 2013.

_____. *Simplicity: The Freedom of Letting God.* Translated by Peter Heinneg. New York: Crossroad Publishing Co., 2003.

_____. *Things Hidden: Scripture and Spirituality.* Cincinnati: St. Anthony Messenger Press, 2008.

_____. *The Naked Now: Learning to See as the Mystics See.* New York: Crossroad Publishing Co., 2009.

Rohr, Richard and John Bookser Feister. *Jesus' Plan for a New World: The Sermon on the Mount.* Cincinnati: St. Anthony Messenger Press, 1996.

_____. *Hope Against Darkness: The Transforming Vision of Saint Francis in an Age of Anxiety.* Cincinnati: St. Anthony Messenger Press, 2001.

Rolheiser, Ronald. *The Holy Longing: The Search for a Christian Spirituality.* New York: Doubleday, 1999.

Rossing, Barbara R. *The Rapture Exposed: The Message of Hope in the Book of Revelation.* Boulder, CO: Westview Press, 2004.

Selmanovic, Samir. *It's Really All About God: Reflections of a Muslim Atheist Jewish Christian.* San Francisco: Jossey-Bass, 2009.

Sobrino, Jon. *Jesus the Liberator: A Historical-Theological Reading of Jesus of Nazareth.* Translated by Paul Burns and Francis McDonagh. Maryknoll, NY: Orbis Books, 2007.

Spong, John Shelby. *A New Christianity for a New World: Why Traditional Faith is Dying and How a New Faith is Being Born.* New York: HarperSanFrancisco, 2001.

_____. *Reclaiming the Bible for a Non-Religious World.* New York: HarperCollins, 2011.

Stark, Thom. *The Human Faces of God: What Scripture Reveals When It Gets God Wrong (and Why Inerrancy Tries To Hide It).* Eugene, OR: Wipf & Stock, 2011.

Steindl-Rast, Brother David. *Deeper than Words: Living the Apostles' Creed.* New York: Doubleday, 2010.

_____. *Gratefulness, the Heart of Prayer: An Approach to Life in Fullness.* New York: Paulist Press, 1984.

Taylor, Barbara Brown. *An Altar in the World: A Geography of Faith.* New York: HarperOne, 2009.

_____. *The Luminous Web: Essays on Science and Religion.* Cambridge: Cowley Publications, 2000.

Tutu, Desmond. *God Has a Dream: A Vision of Hope for Our Time.* New York: Doubleday, 2004.

Vanier, Jean. *Becoming Human.* New York: Paulist Press, 1998.

Wallace, Peter. *The Passionate Jesus: What We Can Learn from Jesus about Love, Fear, Grief, Joy, and Living Authentically.* Woodstock, VT: Skylight Paths Publishing, 2013.

Weaver, J. Denny. *The Nonviolent Atonement.* Grand Rapids / Cambridge: Eerdmans Publishing Co., 2001.

Wellman, Jr., James K. *Rob Bell and a New American Christianity.* Nashville: Abingdon Press, 2012.

Willard, Dallas. *The Divine Conspiracy: Rediscovering Our Hidden Life in God.* New York: HarperSanFrancisco, 1997.

Wills, Garry. *What Jesus Meant.* New York: Viking Press, 2006.

Wink, Walter. *Engaging the Powers: Discernment and Resistance in a World of Domination.* Minneapolis: Augsburg Press, 1992.

————. *Homosexuality and Christian Faith: Questions of Conscience for the Churches.* Edited by Walter Wink. Minneapolis: Fortress Press, 1999

————. *The Powers That Be: Theology for a New Millennium.* New York: Doubleday, 1998.

Wolpe, David J. *Why Faith Matters.* New York: HarperOne, 2008.

Wright, N. T. *Evil and the Justice of God.* Downers Grove, IL: InterVarsity Press, 2006.

————. *Simply Christian: Why Christianity Makes Sense.* New York: HarperSanFrancisco, 2006.

Yancey, Philip. *What's So Amazing About Grace?* Grand Rapids: Zondervan, 1997.